EDEXCEL A-LEVEL/AS RELIGIOUS STUDIES

PAPER 3 NEW TESTAMENT STUDIES

A-LEVEL YEAR 2 RE

Published independently by Tinderspark Press
© Jonathan Rowe 2018

The purchaser of this book is subject to the condition that he/she shall in no way resell it, nor any part of it, nor make copies of it to distribute freely.
All illustrations in this book are Creative Commons. Biblical quotations are from the New International Version UK (NIV-UK).
The author is not affiliated with the Edexcel Exam Board and makes no claim to represent Edexcel's policies, standards or practices.

CONTENTS

4 WAYS OF INTERPRETING THE SCRIPTURE 5

    4.1 SCRIPTURE AS INSPIRED BY GOD 6

    4.1 KARL BARTH: THE 'STORY OF GOD' 8

    4.1 RUDOLF BULTMANN: DEMYTHOLOGIZING SCRIPTURE 9

    4.1 FOUR POST-ENLIGHTENMENT APPROACHES 10

    TOPIC 4 EXAM QUESTIONS & REVISION ACTIVITIES 13

5 KINGDOM OF GOD, CONFLICT, DEATH & RESURRECTION OF JESUS 19

    5.1 THE KINGDOM OF GOD 20

    5.1 PARABLES OF THE KINGDOM (Anthology #5) 21

    5.2 WHY DID JESUS HAVE TO DIE? 24

    5.2 CONFLICT IN JOHN'S GOSPEL (Anthology #6) 25

    5.2 JESUS' ARREST & TRIAL (Anthology #6 cont'd) 28

    5.3 CRUCIFIXION & RESURRECTION IN LUKE (Anthology #7) 31

    TOPIC 5 EXAM QUESTIONS & REVISION ACTIVITIES 36

6 SCIENTIFIC & HISTORICAL-CRITICAL CHALLENGES / ETHICAL LIVING 42

    6.1 CHALLENGES TO THE RESURRECTION 43

    6.1 FRANK MORISON (Anthology #8) 45

    6.1 IAN WILSON (Anthology #9) 46

    3.2 THE SERMON ON THE PLAIN 47

    6.2 ETHICAL PARABLES (Anthology #10) 50

    TOPIC 6 EXAM QUESTIONS & REVISION ACTIVITIES 52

YEAR 2 EXAM PRACTICE PAPER 58

ABOUT THIS BOOK

This book offers notes for teachers and students revising Edexcel A-Level Year 2 Religious Studies, Paper 3 (New Testament Studies). It summarizes the 3 Study Guides which are already available and which greatly expand on the notes in this book.

Topics 4-6 cover the topics in Year 2 of the A-Level. There are 3 study guides detailing these in more depth than this revision guide provides:

  4   Ways of interpreting the scripture
  5   Texts and interpretation: the Kingdom of God, conflict, the death and resurrection of Jesus
  6   Scientific and historical-critical challenges, ethical living and the works of scholars

The AS/A-Level Year 1 topics are covered by 3 study guides and a previous revision guide:

  1   Context of the New Testament
  2   Texts and interpretation of the Person of Jesus
  3   Interpreting the text and issues of relationship, purpose and authorship

Exemplar exam questions are adapted from the specimen papers available to the public on the Edexcel website. The author claims no insight into the content of the actual exam.

Text that is marked like this is a quotation from the Bible. Candidates should use some of these quotations in their exam responses.

Text that is marked like this describes an important episode from the New Testament. Candidates should refer to events in the Gospels to illustrate arguments.

Text that is marked like this is reference to a key scholar. Candidates should link ideas to key scholars wherever possible – underlined passages are the essential part of the quote

Text in this typeface and boxed represents the author's comments, observations and reflections. Such texts are not intended to guide candidates in writing exam answers.

4 WAYS OF INTERPRETING THE SCRIPTURE

4.1 WAYS OF INTERPRETING SCRIPTURE

This topic looks at the idea o**f Scripture as inspired by God** and ways of interpreting Scripture **literally, allegorically** and **morally**; the **debate** between **Barth**'s interpretation of 'The Story of God' and **Bultmann** on de-mythologizing the Bible; **post-Enlightenment approaches** to Biblical interpretation: **rational, historical, sociological** and **literary**. There are no **Key Scholars** in this Topic (although Karl Barth and Rudolf Bultmann take the place of Key Scholars).

KEY TERMINOLOGY:

Allegory: Symbolism where a text has a hidden or non-obvious meaning

Deism: Rationalist religious idea of a God who creates the universe but never intervenes

Dictation: Interpreting Scripture as a word-for-word expression of the Word of God, often using humans as passive mouthpieces

Enlightenment, The: Period in th 18th century when European scholars rejected religion and embraced rational thought, scientific methods and scepticism

Hermeneutics: Theory of how to interpret the Scriptures

Historical: Reinterpreting religious ideas in their historical context

Inerrant: Without any factual or theological mistakes

Inspired: A text whose message (and perhaps wording) is influenced by God

Karl Barth: 20th century German theologian who criticism liberal theology

Liberal: Theology that prefers to treat the Bible symbolically and adapt it to present circumstances

Literal: Straightforward factual meaning without symbolisim or metaphor

Literary: Reinterpreting religious ideas as literary constructs (as poems, narratives, metaphors, personification, etc).

Modernism: Reinterpreting religious ideas in a rationalist, liberal way

Rationalist: Reinterpreting religious ideas non-supernaturally

Rudolf Bultmann: 20th century German theologian who argued for de-mythologizing the Scriptures

Sociological: Reinterpreting religious ideas as products of particular societies or as myths

4.1 SCRIPTURE AS INSPIRED BY GOD

 All Scripture is God-breathed and is useful for teaching, rebuking, correcting and training in righteousness - **2 Timothy 3: 16**

Natural inspiration: not supernatural but deep insight into things, 'only human' and contains mistakes; 'men of their time' = attitudes we reject today (e.g. role of women, slavery); not uniquely inspired (also Jewish **Torah**, the Islamic **Qur'an**)

- **Link to:** modernist theology, **Form Criticism (3.1 Interpreting the Text)**, antisemitism in John's Gospel (**3.2 Audience & Purpose of Fourth Gospel**)

Conceptual inspiration: writers supernaturally influenced = **non-propositional revelation**; divinely inspired thoughts written in normal human way → biases and misunderstandings; **great moral wisdom** + **factual and scientific error**; truths expressed **allegorically**

- **Link to:** liberal theology, Catholic hermeneutics; **Redaction Criticism (3.1 Interpreting the Text)**, contradictions in Gospels (see below)

Dictation theory: God dictated exact wording, writers passively record & do not include own styles/personalities; scripture is INERRANT (no mistakes)

- **Link to:** literal interpretations; opposes Form/Redaction Criticism; **Historical-Grammatical Method** needed to sort out contradictions (see below)

Contradictions: genealogies of Jesus in **Matthew** and **Luke** do not match up; **Luke:** Mary/Joseph go home to Nazareth after Jesus born; **Matthew:** they go to Egypt as refugees; King Herod died 4 BCE (**Matthew**'s birth date) + Quirinius ruled Syria from 6 CE (**Luke**'s birth date)

- **Historical-Grammatical Method:** study history to resolve contradictions (e.g. 2 governors named Quirinius? one Quirinius governed twice?), translate *koine* Greek better (e.g. Luke translates better as Jesus born *before* Quirinius was governor of Syria)
- **King James Version of Bible (1611):** traditional Protestants regard KJV as closest to Word of God (Edexcel uses New International Version (NIV, 2011) in Anthology)

LITERAL INTERPRETATION

Plain or everyday meaning of words; opposite of symbolism/allegorical meaning; Scripture = historical facts: Virgin Birth, miracles, Resurrection; teachings are literal = Heaven, Hell

- Jesus refers to Old Testament verses in a literal way; Jesus' Disciples interpret Jesus literally; e.g. 'Great Commission' (**Matthew 28: 16-20**)
- **Matthew's proof-texts and John's Gospel:** Jesus literally fulfils Scripture

Grammatical Principle identifies figurative language; language not clearly figurative should be interpreted literally; passages can have a spiritual meaning *as well as* being literally true.

Occam's Razor: prefer the simpler explanation (= text is mistaken); however **Source**, **Form** and **Redaction Criticism** just as convoluted and improbable as literal explanations.

ALLEGORICAL INTERPRETATIONS

Secondary or hidden meaning; characters, events, objects, locations are symbolic ;**Origen** (184-253 CE) argues Bible interpreted as "flesh" (**literal**), "soul" (**moral**), "spirit" (**allegorical**).

- **Link to: Topic 3.3 (Miracles & Signs): Turning Water into Wine** (Christianity replacing Judaism. Eucharist), **Healing the Official's Son** (church trusting that God will answer prayers), **Healing at the Pool** (Christianity dispensing with Sabbath regulations), **Feeding the 5000** (Eucharist), **Walking on Water** (faith during times of persecution), **Healing the Blind Man** (spiritual journey of believer/Johannine Community), **Raising Lazarus from the Dead** (the Resurrection, spiritual journey of Johannine Community)

- **Link to: Topic 5.1 (Kingdom of God) & 6.2 (How Should We Live?):** Parables are stories with hidden meaning; e.g **Parable of the Good Samaritan (Luke 10: 30-35)** where victim = humanity; priest/Levite = Judaism; Samaritan = Christ; donkey = Christ's crucified body, inn = church; Samaritan's return = *Parousia* (Second Coming)

- **Anagogical meaning:** refer to the *Eschaton* (end of the world) + *Parousia* (Christ's Second Coming); e.g. wedding party at Cana = heaven/judgement day

GOOD QUOTE — *The literal sense is that which the author intends, but God being the Author, we may expect to find in Scripture a wealth of meaning* – **Thomas Aquinas**

Criticisms: can lead to confusion/self-deception (reading too much into things); Protestant backlash: downplays the historical truth of the Bible, e.g. **Form Criticism** and **Redaction Criticism** → *Sitz im Leben* makes it irrelevant to life in the 21st century

MORAL INTERPRETATION

Tropological interpretation involving ethical guidance; linked to *midrash* in Judaism (a commentary on Scripture drawing out moral meaning); also in Christianity, e.g. **Paul** writes:

everything that was written in the past was written to teach us – **Romans 15: 4**

Link: Topic 3.3 (Miracles & Signs): Sign of Feeding the 5000: non-supernatural miracle of sharing: we share our own possessions → collectively we have enough for everyone; **Pope Francis**: *"This is the miracle: rather than a multiplication, it is a sharing"*

Jesus heals Jairus' daughter, who seemed to be dead, by saying *"Talitha koum"* (which means, 'Little girl, I say to you, get up!')" – **Mark 5: 41**

"Maiden, arise!" (in older translations) became a slogan for Suffragettes and women's colleges in 20th century. Adds new depths to Christian ethical teachings on women's rights vs **eisegesis** (reading your own ideas INTO the Bible rather than taking God's ideas OUT of the Bible)

4.1 KARL BARTH: THE 'STORY OF GOD'

Karl Barth: Swiss theologian; disillusioned with liberal/modernist Christianity (many liberal Christians supported German military aggression); *Church Dogmatics* (1931); helped found German Confessing Church to oppose Nazi ideology: choose between Jesus Christ and Adolf Hitler as Lord

Rejection of Idolatry: (sin of worshiping something else instead of God: → "NO!" to natural theology (e.g. **Design, Cosmological** and **Ontological Arguments**, 'Quest for the Historical Jesus', **Source, Form** and **Redaction Criticism**) → Idolatry because they substitute human ideas for God

One can not speak of God simply by speaking of man in a loud voice - **Karl Barth**
It is by the grace of God that God is knowable to us - **Karl Barth**

Grace & Revelation: 'Grace' = anything God gives to humans without them asking for it or earning it; need God to **reveal** himself to humans → there is no revelation outside of Jesus Christ

The fact that we know God is His work and not ours - **Karl Barth**

Scripture as a Witness: *God's Search for Man* (1935): title sums up Barth's view on Grace; God finds us when we read the Bible → Bible as WITNESS + Church as PROCLAMATION of Jesus Christ to the world; both human institutions with "*capacity for error*" (= Bible/Church not INERRANT)

The Bible is God's Word to the extent that God causes it to be His Word - **Karl Barth**
Scripture does indeed bear witness to revelation, but it is not revelation itself - **Karl Barth**

We need to allow Bible to **become** Word of God for us when we read it vs turning it into an idol or a *"paper Pope"* to be blindly obeyed

'Story of God': Bible should be read as story rather than facts/history → you can encounter God within the story vs only encounter own thoughts and reflections; two events in history which are "*unhistorical history*" = creation of universe + Resurrection (no one was there to see it; unimaginable, not like normal history - yet they happened_.

Strengths: corrects errors of Liberal/Modernist Christianity; insights gave him wisdom and courage to oppose Nazism; says get society to fit with Bible, opposing interpret Bible to fit society

Criticisms: traditional/conservative Christians regard Bible as INERRANT (**Chicago Statement, 1978**); Barth seems to go against rational analysis and logical thought; Liberals see Barth as a conservative opposed to new interpretations of the Bible/Christian ethics

4.1 RUDOLF BULTMANN: DEMYTHOLOGIZING SCRIPTURE

Rudolf Bultmann: German theologian; key scholar for **Form Criticism**; (*Gospel of John: A Commentary*, 1941); member of the **Confessing Church** that opposed Nazism; 1950s lecture tours turned into influential books (*Jesus Christ & Mythology*, 1958); inspired the 'Bultmann School' of scholarship

Mythological World View: early Christians had MYTHOLOGICAL WORLD VIEW vs modern SCIENTIFIC WORLD VIEW (e.g. 'triple-decker' universe of heaven/earth/hell, miracles, evil spirits, world is coming to an end)

We cannot use electric lights and radios and, in the event of illness, avail ourselves of modern medical and clinical means and at the same time believe in the spirit and wonder world of the New Testament – **Rudolf Bultmann**

For modern people, mythological view is "*over and done with*"; keeping it is *sacrificium intellectus* (sacrificing your understanding) and this is "*pointless and impossible*"

Christian Existentialism: inspired by Heidegger; need to live an AUTHENTIC life without fear or anxiety → 'Word of God' is really a programme for authentic living

Jesus demands truthfulness and purity, readiness to sacrifice and to love – **Rudolf Bultmann**

De-mythologizing: Bultmann wants to draw attention to the REAL 'Word of God' in the Bible → solution to modern life BUT disentangle the 'Word of God' from mythology surrounding it:

= **discarding the mythological elements of a story to make the underlying meaning clearer**

Meaning = *kerygma* (original Christian preaching); Christians de-mythologized early APOCALYPTIC belief in end of the world; replaced it with idea of **Eternal Life**

De-mythologizing has its beginning in the New Testament itself, and therefore our task of de-mythologizing today is justified – **Rudolf Bultmann**

Virgin Birth and other miracles are mythological and should **not be taken literally**; Resurrection is a myth; we should *as if* Bible stories are true vs trying to convince themselves they actually happened

Strengths: influenced by **Karl Barth**'s criticisms of liberal theology → rescue liberal theology because Christian *kerygma* still has value: it is myth-with-a-meaning

Criticisms: modern people may not be scientific (68% of Americans believe in literal Devil); under-estimates evidence for historical Jesus; logical conclusion is to treat *kerygma* as a myth too (why not base life on popular movies instead?); existentialism is out-of-date in ethics

4.1 FOUR POST-ENLIGHTENMENT APPROACHES

Enlightenment: "Age of Reason"; **Descartes** (17th century) → American/French Revolutions (late 18th century); European thinkers rejected earlier beliefs/traditions → new ways of looking at the world (philosophy, science, politics)

Rationalism: power of reason tests all ideas; questions religion, especially inconsistencies and contradictions → DEISM (belief in a more rational God than the one in the Bible)

GOOD QUOTE	*SAPERE AUDE! 'Have courage to use your own reason!' - that is the motto of Enlightenment* – **Immanuel Kant** (18th century)

- **Deism:** belief in non-interventionist God; would not do irrational things described in Bible
- **European Wars of Religion** (17th century): Catholics vs Protestants; huge bloodshed (battles + executions for heresy & witchcraft); Enlightenment thinkers horrified by this; appeal of Deism as it wouldn't lead to atrocities

GOOD QUOTE	*a religion that would foster moral unity rather than immoral hostility within and among human societies* – **Merold Westphal** (20th century)

Empiricism: all knowledge comes from experience of world using 5 senses; **Francis Bacon** argued for a scientific worldview based on empiricism; **Isaac Newton** developed laws of physics; appeals to **Deism** (God exists but does not intervene since world operates by laws)

Scepticism: doubting truth of all knowledge claims; **David Hume** questioned **miracles** and the classical **arguments for the existence of God**; **Voltaire** mocked churches and exposed religious hypocrisy; caused many thinkers to abandon Christianity in favour of **Deism** or atheism.

- **Thomas Hobbes** (1651): questioned whether Moses really wrote first five books of Old Testament (*Pentateuch*)
- **Jean Astruc** (1753): used literary analysis to show **Book of Genesis** was not written by one person; several sources combined together to form the text = **Source Criticism**
- **Baron D'Holbach** (1761): exposes illogicality of entire Bible: calls the Old Testament "*a tissue of fables and allegories, incapable of giving any true idea of things*" and uses contradictions between Gospels to question whether they were **inspired** by God

GOOD QUOTE	Bible is more likely to be "*the work of a malign spirit, a genius of darkness and falsehood, than of a God desirous to preserve, enlighten and beautify mankind*" – **Baron D'Holbach**

Strengths: major development in philosophical thought; forced religious thinkers to respond with better arguments and re-examine their assumptions; tested traditional beliefs

Criticisms: introduced hostility to religion; not all atheism based on sound arguments; rejected much that was positive about religion along with much that was inconsistent (e.g. mysticism)

RATIONAL APPROACH

Based on **Deism**: *"the religion of the Enlightenment"* (**Merold Westphal**); rejects revealed religions and need for churches/priests; **universalist religion** which can appeal to all humans

Implications: rejects miracles, spirits, visions and supernatural events; real ministry of Jesus distorted or exaggerated by the churches; tries to reconstruct Jesus as a moral teacher

Criticisms: David Hume and Immanuel Kant challenged arguments for existence of God; **Design Argument** by **Charles Darwin**'s theory of evolution → Deism declined in popularity

EXAMPLE: HERMANN REIMARUS (1694-1768): Deist; wrote attack on Christianity published after his death as *Wolfenbüttel Fragments*; distinguishes between what Jesus actually said/did and what Disciples *claimed* he said/did → difference between 'Jesus of history' vs 'Christ of faith'

- **Reimarus' Jesus:** started off as preacher who respected **Jewish Law**; turned into political revolutionary against Romans; executed by the Romans because he really was a rebel; Disciples stole his body and faked Resurrection

Implications: tries to demolish Christianity → prove Deism true; **Matthew 28: 15** refers to rumour that Disciples stole Jesus' body; ahead of his time (pioneers type of **Form Criticism**)

Criticisms: this black-and-white view treats Bible as lies and stupidity; 'Theft Hypothesis' rejected by **David Strauss** (1836); in **Topic 6.1 (Challenges to Resurrection) Frank Morison** argues it is unlikely Disciples carried out hoax since they were persecuted for their beliefs;

HISTORICAL APPROACH

Tries to identify true events behind Bible texts; NOT arguing for a Deist interpretation; known as "Higher Criticism"; includes **Synoptic Problem, Source, Form** and **Redaction Criticism**; seeks insight into *"the world **behind** the text"*

Implications: need to study *"the world **of** the text"* (ancient languages, archaeology, etc); inconsistencies reveal author's agenda; helps expose ANACHRONISM (projecting later religious beliefs onto Jesus & Disciples, e.g. link to **Topic 1 (Prophecies Concerning the Messiah)** Wrede's theory of **Messianic Secret** = historical Jesus never claimed to be Messiah)

Criticism: REVISIONIST (always trying to revise our understanding of Jesus) = **Albert Schweitzer** (1906) argues 'Historical Jesus' really based on Enlightenment values; ignores *"the world **in front of** the text"* = what Bible means mean for people reading it today (link to **Karl Barth** 'Story of God', **Rudolf Bultmann** de-mythologizing Bible for scientific age.

EXAMPLE: F.C. BAUR (1792-1860): founder of Higher Criticism; Bible conceals conflict between **Paul**'s (**Pauline**) Gentile version of Christianity vs **Peter**'s (**Petrine**) Jewish version; these opposing sides united in *synthesis* as Gospels were being written → merging formed religion of Christianity: **universalistic** (could appeal to everyone) but kept Jewish Old Testament

Implications: Christianity turned out very different from what (Jewish) Jesus intended

Criticisms: weakened by decline of Hegelian idea of historical progress through opposing ideas; ; two opposing ideas is simplistic (LOTS of competing groups, e.g. Johannine Community)

SOCIOLOGICAL APPROACH

Compare Christianity to other world religions (Islam, Hinduism, Buddhism) and to so-called primitive religions → a 'religious impulse' in mankind; similarities between religious ideas; focus on myths and symbols that recur in religions

Implications: Christianity began as a 'cult'; Romans persecuted it but **Rodney Stark** (1965) argues that Christianity triumphed because it offered people a sense of meaning

Criticisms: Ignores specific Christian teachings (e.g. agape-love) and importance of particular Christian figures (e.g. Paul converting Gentiles)

EXAMPLE: SIR JAMES FRAZER (1854-1941): wrote *The Golden Bough* (1915) = massive 12-volume study of myths and legends from around the world; common belief in a **dying-and-rising god** (maybe symbolises planting → harvest, winter → spring)) e.g. **Osiris** (Egyptian) =**Jesus**

Implications: myths are memories of ancient magical rituals OR symbolise agricultural process (harvest → winter → spring); Christianity = another myth; Jesus = dying-and-rising god linked to harvest ('**Bread of Life**')

Criticisms: 'armchair researcher' who never went to any of the tribal societies he described; purely speculative; **C.S. Lewis** argues Christianity is "*a myth which is also a fact*"

LITERARY APPROACH

Narrative Theology focuses on Bible as literature; use of symbolism and metaphor; downplays Bible as source of **PROPOSITIONS** (laws e.g. 'love your neighbour') vs focus on **NARRATIVES** (stories, e.g. Crucifixion, Resurrection); **Clark Pinnock** (2000) calls Bible *"theodrama"* (story of God's involvement with mankind – link to **Karl Barth**, 'Story of God')

Implications: narrative is not an unnecessary fairy tale - it's vital; Jesus told stories (**parables**) but if propositions could have made the point better, Jesus would have expressed himself that way; e.g. "God is love" revealed through Jesus suffering on the Cross (**Matthew 27: 32-56**)

Criticisms: rejects Bible being **INERRANT** (without error) – important belief for conservative Christians; makes propositions subjective (a matter of opinion)

EXAMPLE: C.S. LEWIS (1898-1963): professor of English Literature who specialised in myths/legends; *Myth Became Fact* (1944) argues that it's impossible to get propositions out of the Bible while ignoring the narrative:

> **GOOD QUOTE** *in the enjoyment of a great myth we come nearest to experiencing as a concrete what can otherwise be understood only as an abstraction* – **C.S. Lewis**

Implications: Lewis says we "*feed*" on myth because myth expresses deeper truths than propositions; even scientific theories (e.g. evolution) are myths; criticism of **Bultmann** who wants to de-mythologize Christianity

Criticisms: Proposition that Jesus is Lord and Saviour is essential for most Christians; atheists can be moved by Gospel story but that doesn't mean they will go to Heaven if they deny Jesus/God

A-Level Year 2 New Testament Studies

TOPIC 4 EXAM QUESTIONS & REVISION ACTIVITIES

A-Level Paper 3 (New Testament)

Section A

1. Explore key ideas regarding the sociological approach to interpreting the Bible. (8 marks)
2. Assess the significance of the view that the Bible is inspired by God. (12 marks)

Section B

Read the following passage before answering the questions.

Jesus Has Risen

²⁴ On the first day of the week, very early in the morning, the women took the spices they had prepared and went to the tomb.² They found the stone rolled away from the tomb, ³ but when they entered, they did not find the body of the Lord Jesus. ⁴ While they were wondering about this, suddenly two men in clothes that gleamed like lightning stood beside them. ⁵ In their fright the women bowed down with their faces to the ground, but the men said to them, "Why do you look for the living among the dead? ⁶ He is not here; he has risen! Remember how he told you, while he was still with you in Galilee: ⁷ 'The Son of Man must be delivered over to the hands of sinners, be crucified and on the third day be raised again.' " ⁸ Then they remembered his words.

⁹ When they came back from the tomb, they told all these things to the Eleven and to all the others. ¹⁰ It was Mary Magdalene, Joanna, Mary the mother of James, and the others with them who told this to the apostles. ¹¹ But they did not believe the women, because their words seemed to them like nonsense. ¹² Peter, however, got up and ran to the tomb. Bending over, he saw the strips of linen lying by themselves, and he went away, wondering to himself what had happened.

Quote from New International Translation, Luke 24: 1-17

3. (a) Clarify the ideas of Rudolf Bultmann on de-mythologizing the text illustrated by this passage. *You must refer to the passage in your response.* (10 marks)

   (b) Assess the claim that stories in the Gospels cannot be believed by modern people with a scientific world view. (20 marks)

Section C

4 Evaluate the view that the Bible should be interpreted allegorically.

In your response to this question, you must include how developments in New Testament Studies have been influenced by one of the following:

- Philosophy of Religion
- Religion and Ethics
- the study of a religion.

(30 marks)

Total = 90 marks

In this example paper, all the questions are drawn from Topic 4 (although the Anthology passage is from Topic 5, since there's no Anthology extract linked to Topic 4). A real exam would not be like this and each question would probably draw from a different Topic instead.

Comprehension Quiz

1. What is meant by inspired scriptures?
2. What is the difference between a conceptual and a dictation view of inspired scriptures?
3. What is allegory?
4. Give an example of a moral interpretation of scripture
5. What is the difference between a conservative and a liberal Christian?
6. Why does Karl Barth oppose liberal theology?
7. What does Barth mean by the Bible as a witness to God's revelation?
8. In what way is Rudolf Bultmann 'rescuing' liberal theology?
9. What does Bultmann mean by de-mythologizing Christianity?
10. Who was the Enlightenment?
11. What is the difference between Deism and Christianity?
12. What was Reimarus' view of the historical Jesus?
13. What is the Higher Criticism?
14. What is a myth?
15. What's the difference between a propositions and narratives?

Bible/Scholar Quotes to match

Explain how each quote links to this Topic

1. *All Scripture is God-breathed and is useful for teaching, rebuking, correcting and training in righteousness* – **2 Timothy 3: 16**
2. *"I am the Bread of Life"* – **John 6: 35**
3. *everything that was written in the past was written to teach us* – **Romans 15: 4**
4. *"Talitha koum!" (which means "Little girl, I say to you, get up!")* – **Mark 5: 41**
5. *One can not speak of God simply by speaking of man in a loud voice* – **Karl Barth**
6. *It is by the grace of God that God is knowable to us* – **Karl Barth**
7. *We cannot use electric lights and radios and, in the event of illness, avail ourselves of modern medical and clinical means and at the same time believe in the spirit and wonder world of the New Testament* – **Rudolf Bultmann**
8. *Jesus demands truthfulness and purity, readiness to sacrifice and to love* – **Rudolf Bultmann**

Revision Guide 2

Word Search

Find 20 terms/names from this Topic and explain them

```
G C E N H S D V Y J D H N L A
Y N L N R O D F W P T S A J B
R O I A L C J C X E E C L J T
T G T M N I N G V T I A L I Q
A C E T Y O G C D R C K E W Y
L D R L Y L I H O I S V G N G
O E A U B O C T T N H D O Y O
D H L B J G S P A E E T R Z L
I U A M S I E D P R N A Y I O
B A R T H C V A I A R M B M P
O B O R S A U P C E X E E F O
K F M T P L S E T Q R J A N R
Z Y P H I N O I M A O D I N T
S B R N I J L L L Z O X Q M D
C K E R Y G M A L A W F P N T
```

Crossword

Across
1. Karl Barth says this is what the Bible is
3. German theologian who demythologized Christianity
5. Swiss theologian who rejected liberal theology
7. A story with a meaning that isn't factual
8. When God determines the exact wording of Scripture
10. Something you worship instead of God
11. Wrote 'The Golden Bough'
14. Egyptian god who died and rose to life
15. A type of theology prepared interpret Scripture to fit into the modern world

Down
2. The 'Age of Reason'
4. When a text comes from God
6. Belief in a non-interventionist God
9. Reading a hidden meaning into a text
12. Wrote the Wolfenbüttel Fragments
13. The straightforward, factual interpretation

Debates in this Topic

Indicate where you stand on this debate by marking a cross on the line then list points in favour and points against your position (more in favour the closer to the edge, more against the closer to the middle)

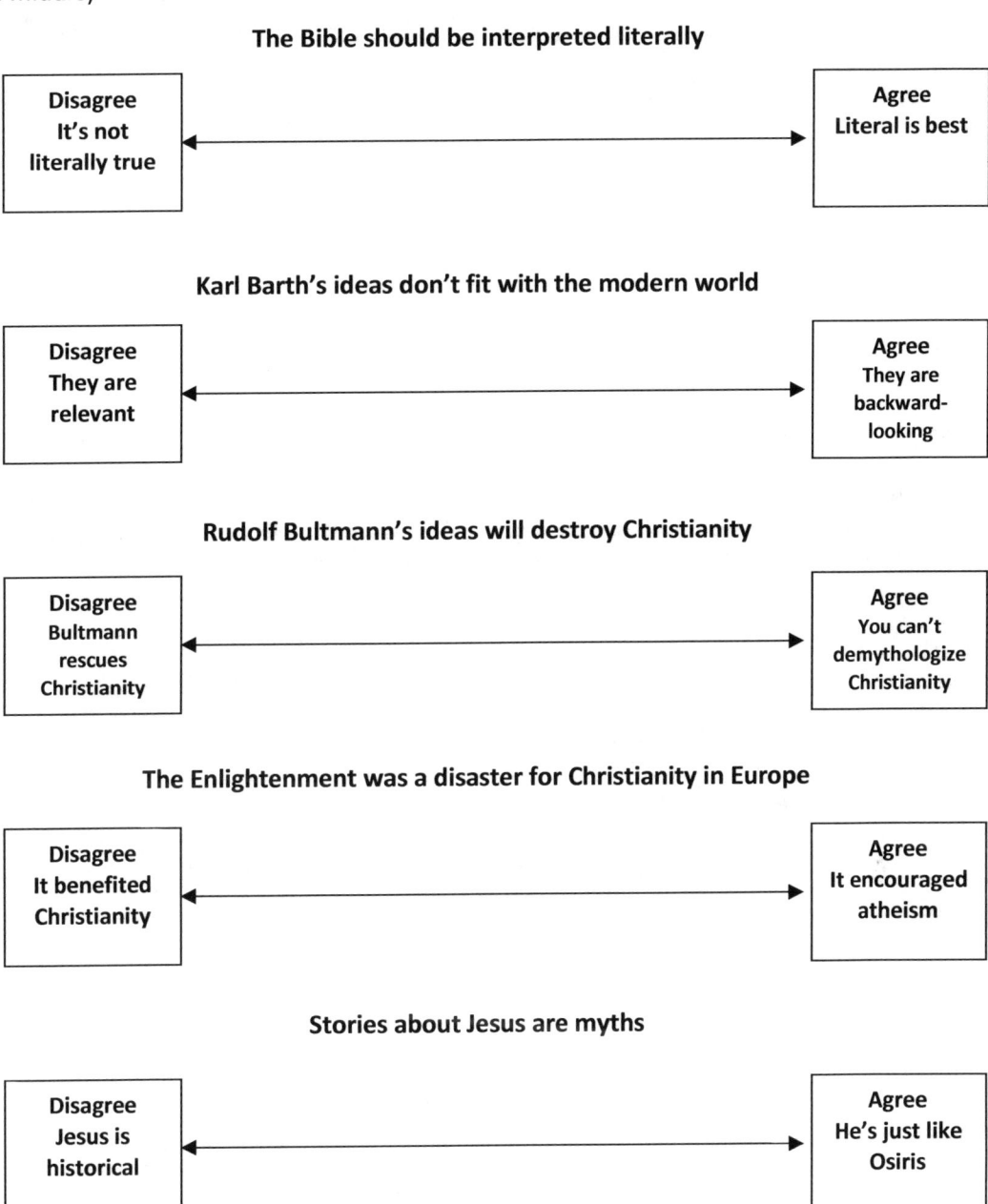

Cloze Exercise

Christians considered the Bible to be divinely _____ or "God-breathed". This means God has influenced what is in it. _____ theory suggests that God has influenced every word of the Bible, which makes the Bible _____ (without mistakes). However, _____ inspiration means that God has influenced the ideas in the Bible but not the precise way they are expressed, which leaves room for human error. _____ tend to take the first view and argue society should fit in with the Bible, whereas liberals take the second view and interpret the Bible to fit in with society, e.g. by contextualizing things like hostility to homosexuality and the equality of women in the Bible as the writers being "_____".

If every word of the Bible is factually true, then the Bible should be interpreted _____. This leads to contradictions, such as the different details of the birth-narratives in _____ and Luke. Christians can use the _____ method to 'explain away' these inconsistencies. However, many Christians treat Bible stories as _____ which have a hidden meaning. For example, the visit of the Magi to the baby Jesus could symbolise _____ recognizing who Christ is when Jews do not.

_____ was opposed to liberal theology, because he saw many liberals supporting German aggression in the World Wars of the 20th century. He argued that using our intellects to build up our own idea of God is a form of _____. Instead, he argued that Jesus is the only revelation of what God is like, the Bible is a _____ to that revelation and the church a _____ of that revelation. This means we must read the Bible so that God can encounter us.

However, _____ took a different view. He thought the _____ word-view of the Bible was completely unacceptable to modern people who have a _____ world-view. He suggested the Bible must be _____ to reveal its core message, which is an _____ ethical philosophy about how to live an authentic life without fear and anxiety.

All of these ideas follow on from the _____ in the 18th century, which changed the way scholars view the Bible. This was the 'Age of _____' when thinkers rejected irrational traditions in favour of _____ evidence. Many philosophers were Deists who still believed in God, but not one who would _____ in nature or do the immoral things the Bible describes.

This period produced four main approaches to interpreting Scriptures. The _____ approach exposed nonsensical material in the Bible to support a Deist interpretation; the historical approach (also known as '_____') explored the circumstances in which the Bible came to be written and the original beliefs of Jesus and his Disciples; the sociological approach treats stories about Jesus as _____; and the literary approach focuses on the Bible as a story that reveals _____ truths through _____.

allegories, conceptual, conservatives, de-mythologized, dictation, empirical, Enlightenment, existential, Gentiles, Higher Criticism, historical-grammatical, idolatry, inerrant, Inspired, intervene, Karl Barth, literally, Matthew, men of their time, mythological, myths, narrative, proclamation, propositional, rational Reason, Rudolf Bultmann, scientific, witness

5 KINGDOM OF GOD, CONFLICT, DEATH & RESURRECTION OF JESUS

5.1 KINGDOM OF GOD

This topic looks at the idea of the **Kingdom of God** in Luke's Gospel, the **Parables** that explore this and the different theories of **Eschatology** (past, present or future). Key scholars are **I. Howard Marshall** & **Albert Schweitzer**

5.2 WHY DID JESUS HAVE TO DIE?

This topic covers Jesus' **conflict** with the authorities in the Fourth Gospel, his **arrest** and **trial**, with reference to **charges** against him regarding the **Law, Temple cleansing** and **Sabbath controversies, Christology** & **blasphemy, threat to power** & **expediency**. Key scholars are **Ellis Rivkin** and **R. Alan Culpepper**.

5.3 DEATH & RESURRECTION OF JESUS

This topic covers the **Crucifixion** and **Resurrection** narratives in Luke, with reference to **the Old Testament** and **fulfillment of Scripture, sacrifice, salvation & atonement, power of God, forgiveness of sins & relationship with God**. Key scholars are **I. Howard Marshall** & **Frank Matera**.

KEY TERMINOLOGY:

Apocalypticism: belief in the end of the world being imminent (about to happen)

Apocalypse: Revelation of God's Kingdom in a sudden transformation (Judgment Day)

Atonement: Paying for sin through your own death and/or suffering

Blasphemy: Saying or doing things that insult God

Christology: Beliefs about whether Jesus is a holy human person or a divine being in human form

Crucifixion: Roman method of executing outlaws, rebels and escaped slaves; considered deeply shameful way to die by Romans and crucified victims were considered cursed by Jews

Eschatological: referring either to the end of the world (**Apocalypse**) or the Afterlife

Kingdom: or Kingdom of God; state of affairs where God rules humans (on Earth or in Afterlife)

Sabbath: Jewish day of rest on which work is forbidden

Salvation History: View of Jesus' ministry as the culmination of Jewish history and the beginning of a new Christian period in history, with the Apocalypse in the far future

Sanhedrin: Ruling council of Jewish priests

Temple: Massive place of Jewish worship in Jerusalem where animals were sacrificed according to the regulations in the Torah; destroyed by the Romans in 70 CE

5.1 THE KINGDOM OF GOD

Kingdom of God: Jesus' original *kerygma* (preaching); features in all four Gospels (**Matthew** substitutes 'Kingdom of Heaven'. **John** prefers **Eternal Life**); 39 references in **Luke's Gospel**

'Kingdom of God' should be taken to refer primarily to <u>God's sovereignty rather than to the realm over which he is sovereign</u> – **I. Howard Marshall**

Kingdom in the past: literal kingdom; God made Israelites his Chosen People; David's Kingdom (c. 1000 BCE) was ideal Jewish state; some good kings of Judah ruled over Kingdom of God; Kingdom of God destroyed by Babylonians in 589 BCE; Kingly Messiah might restore it

Kingdom in the present: spiritual/symbolic kingdom; something happening during Jesus' ministry

The coming of the kingdom of God is not something that can be observed, nor will people say, 'Here it is,' or 'There it is,' because the kingdom of God is in your midst – **Luke 17: 20-21**

Kingdom in the future: literal (if on Earth) or symbolic (if in Afterlife); arrives at the end of the age; 'Second Coming' of Christ (*Parousia*); Judgement Day; could be IMMINENT (in the future, but soon) or REMOTE (in the far future); both themes present in **Luke**

Realised Eschatology: C.H. Dodd argues Jesus taught Kingdom was spiritual and occurring during his ministry, not an event in the future/afterlife; argues references to future events in **Luke** are **allegorical**; opposed by **I.H. Marshall**.

Preterist Eschatology: Albert Schweitzer argues 1st century Christians expected Second Coming (*Parousia*) to be imminent but it did not happen; Jesus makes 'embarrassing' prediction:

this generation will certainly not pass away until all these things (i.e. the end of the world) *have happened* – **Luke 21: 32**

Parousia Delay: Parousia did not happen in 1st century; later Gospels postpone or remove futurist eschatology (end of the world is in far future or replaced with **Eternal Life** now):

no one can see the kingdom of God unless they are born again – **John 3: 3**

Salvation-History: Conzelmann (1954) suggests **Luke** reinterprets Kingdom in a historical sense: 'Age of Israel' ends with Jesus → Jesus' ministry → 'Age of Church' is new age following after

Jesus taught the Apocalypse is:		
Immediate	**Imminent**	**Future**
Schweitzer (literal) **C.H. Dodd** (symbolic, personal transformation)	**Marshall** (symbolic & literal, e.g. founding of church & destruction of Jerusalem in 70 CE)	**Conzelmann** (symbolic & literal, e.g. the Afterlife & Judgement Day in the far future)

5.1 PARABLES OF THE KINGDOM (Anthology #5)

Parables = stories told by Jesus with a spiritual meaning

- **Form Criticism** = these are *PERICOPAE* or textual units reflecting beliefs about KoG (Kingdom of God) of 1st century Christians (not necessarily Jesus' original teachings)
- **Redaction Criticism** = these have been edited by Luke to support viewpoint of Gospel-writer (i.e. **Luke** promotes salvation-history, explains '*Parousia* delay')

THE PARABLE OF THE SOWER (Luke 8: 1-15)

Introduction: Jesus' diverse followers (Twelve Disciples + Mary Magdalene + other women); Parable explains why some enter KoG but others do not

Plot: Farmer sows by scattering seed; seed lands on (1) path (eaten by birds), (2) rocky ground (withered in sun), (3) thorns (choked by weeds), (4) good soil (yielded crop x100)

Meaning: seed = Word of God; soil = different listeners/converts; (1) *path* = unspiritual people, (2) *rocky ground* = shallow people, (3) *thorns* = worldly pressures (e.g. job, money) getting in the way of religion, (4) *good soil* = ideal listeners: attentive and deep, those who persevere

Implications: no reference to the Apocalypse or *Parousia*; KoG is inside hearts of believers; reference to persecutions of 1st century Christians; fits in with **Conzelmann**'s idea of salvation-history BUT this is in ALL the Synoptics so it supports **Marshall**'s view that Luke has *not* altered the earliest traditions about KoG

JESUS & BEELZEBUB (Luke 11: 14-28)

Introduction: Beelzebub = pagan god, name for the Devil; Jesus heals mute man by driving out evil spirit (EXORCISM); Jesus accused of serving Devil; denies this by saying he has God's authority over devils because he is part of KoG

Plot (Parable of Strong Man): strong man guards his house; robber breaks in and overpowers him and steals his belongings; **(Parable of 7 Devils):** spirit is cast out of house but returns with 7 more; they overpower the human and live in his house/body

Meaning: house = soul of a person (or else Jewish nation or Jerusalem Temple); strong man = human moral code or Jewish **Law** which are ineffective; robber = Devil (or Roman Army destroying Temple); 7 devils = power of sin which only Jesus can defeat

Implications: only Jesus has the power to drive out Satan once and for all; goodness/Law is ineffective; (1) link to **Conzelmann**'s salvation-history = Christians must continue war against Satan themselves; (2) link to **Marshall**'s imminent Apocalypse = devils taking over house predicts destruction of Jerusalem in 70 CE; (3) link to **Dodd**'s Realised Eschatology = *"the kingdom of God has come upon you"* suggests KoG is in the present

THE SIGN OF JONAH (Luke 11: 29-32)

Introduction: Jonah = prophet sent by God to warn sinful people of **Nineveh** (Babylon) about destruction; Ninevites repent so God spares them; **Queen of the South** = 'Queen of Sheba' who visits King Solomon (the son of King David) to test his wisdom

Plot: (1) *men of Nineveh* listened to Jonah; (2) *Queen of the South* listened to Solomon; but (3) Jewish audience won't listen to Jesus though he is greater than any prophet

Meaning: listeners are like the *path* or the *rocky ground* in **Parable of the Sower (PoS)**: they hear Jesus preach but don't take the message seriously

Implications: tone of urgency links to *Parousia* happening imminently (**Marshall**'s view) BUT Luke seems to have **redacted** this (removing reference to Crucifixion/Resurrection found in **Matthew**) so just a general warning ('one day' but not necessarily 'soon' – **Conzelmann**); people of Nineveh were *not* destroyed because God is merciful → explains to Christians why Apocalypse postponed

THE NARROW DOOR (Luke 13: 22-30)

Introduction: Parable is unique to Luke, although **Matthew 7: 13-14** warns about broad gate to Hell and narrow gate to Heaven; **John 10: 7-9** refers to Jesus as Door/Gate to **Eternal Life**

Plot: (1) People try to enter a house but owner locks it and they are left outside begging to get in; (2) they insist they are friends of the owner but he doesn't know them and sends them away

Meaning: *owner of the house* = God; those who *stand outside knocking* = souls being judged; being sent away = Hell; link to **PoS** (people heard Jesus' preaching and *received the word with joy* but the KoG didn't grow in them because they weren't sincere)

Implications: Tone of urgency but non-specific about timing (imminent or in the future? or Afterlife?) – could support either **Conzelmann** or **Marshall**; maybe house = 1st century church closing door to people who returned to paganism during persecutions

PARABLE OF GRAND BANQUET (Luke 14: 15-24)

Introduction: Parable also occurs in **Matthew 22: 1-14**, but Luke's version does not feature the wedding banquet of a king's son (= Christ being raised up as God's Son)

Plot: Man organizes a banquet but invited guests don't want to attend so he (1) invites poor people from the streets, then (2) fills up places with people from out-of-town

Meaning: party host = God; banquet = KoG; original guests = Jews; servant = Jesus Christ; poor people = outcast Jews (e.g. Publicans, women); country people = Gentiles

Implication: **Matthew**'s version has APOCALYPTIC tone (servants = prophets, ungrateful guests are killed); Luke removes this apocalyptic material → focuses on worldly reasons guests have for refusing invitation (link to different types of soil in **PoS**) → **Conzelmann**'s idea of salvation-history (banquet is Afterlife not end of the world); invitation to *the poor, the crippled, the blind and the lame* = Luke's social concerns with sharing wealth

THE COMING OF THE KINGDOM (Luke 17: 20-37)

Introduction: This is a discourse (speech) on the Apocalypse, similar to one in **Matthew 24**

Plot: Jesus says that *"the Kingdom of God is in your midst"*; he predicts that there will be rumours about the Apocalypse but followers are not to believe them because the Son of Man (cosmic judge and redeemer) will be *"like the lightning"* (i.e. appear suddenly; comparisons to 'mini-apocalypses' of **Noah** and **Lot**

Meaning: (1) KoG = spiritual state not physical reality (**Conzelmann**); (2) KoG is happening in the present moment (Jesus is literally standing in the midst of the crowd - **Marshall**); Noah's Flood and destruction of city of Sodom (Lot's home) took everyone by surprise

Implications: Warning against expecting imminent Apocalypse; Jesus adds *"but first…"* = his own Passion (death/Resurrection) must occur → KoG isn't appearing right away.

THE RICH & THE KINGDOM OF GOD (Luke 18: 18-20)

Introduction: Wealthy ruler wants to enter KoG; Jesus says keep Ten Commandments; ruler replies that he keeps all the Commandments

Plot: Jesus tells give wealth to the poor and become a Disciple; ruler doesn't want to; Jesus concludes it's easier for camel to go through eye of needle than for rich man to enter KoG

Meaning: ruler = *rocky soil* in **PoS**: not deep enough to appreciate KoG; wealth = *thorns* in **PoS**; (1) *kamêlos* ("camel") is mistranslation of *kamilos* ("rope"), or (2) 'the Needle's Eye' = narrow gate into Jerusalem, must unload camel of goods to enter

Implications: earliest Christians shared possessions communally; later Christians argued you should be ***prepared*** to give up all your wealth; *age to come* started to mean the Afterlife, rather than the Apocalypse (=**Conzelmann**'s idea of salvation-history; **Marshall** points out this is also in Mark, so Luke didn't alter the original passage to fit a new anti-apocalyptic way of thinking)

THE PARABLE OF THE TEN MINAS (Luke 19: 11-27)

Introduction: also in **Matthew 25: 14-30** but from different source (e.g. *talents* instead of *minas*)

Plot: Noble goes away to be crowned king; leaves 10 servants with one *mina* or money (= 50 shekels); nobleman (now a king) returns; those who invested are rewarded; servant who did not invest is punished and his money given to successful servant

Meaning: Noble = Jesus (leaving to become king = Ascension, return = *Parousia*); servants = Church; *minas* = Word of God (similar to seed in **PoS**)

Implications: wicked servant = Jews who treat God as a *hard man* (fear God, not love him); OR = Christian converts who lose interest or backslide during persecutions; link to salvation-history = Christians waiting for *Parousia* → those who commit to the Christian life will be rewarded.

5.2 WHY DID JESUS HAVE TO DIE?

RELIGIOUS & POLITICAL AUTHORITIES

High Priest & Sanhedrin: High Priest = **Joseph Caiaphas** (Sadducee appointed by Romans to collaborate with them, ally of **Pontius Pilate**); needed to keep the peace and prevent rebellion; Sanhedrin = 'parliament' of Jewish leaders

> **Ellis Rivkin** argues that Sanhedrin was a POLITICAL council not a religious body; religious council was a BET DIN (no political authority)

Sadducees: sect of wealthy and conservative Jews; rejected beliefs of the Pharisees (such as life after death); maintained Temple and sacrifices described in Torah; idea of the Temple being destroyed was threat to status and wealth as well as their religion.

Pharisees: largest sect; believed in life after death (so long as Law followed precisely); threatened by religious movement telling people they didn't need to follow the Pharisees' laws

Roman Empire: wanted taxes and law and order; governor = **Pontius Pilate** (since 26 CE); harsh, stubborn man; executing troublemakers → riots and revolt; guided by **Caiaphas the High Priest**

JESUS' CONFLICT WITH THE AUTHORITIES

(1) Christology: beliefs about Jesus' relationship with God; idea that Jesus is God = **blasphemy** for Jewish authorities; **Son of God** is POLITICAL claim for Romans (rival to the Emperor)

(2) Blasphemy: Law of Moses sentences those who insult God to death; attacks on the Temple (home of God) or Torah (Word of God for Jews); breaking **Pharisee** rules on Sabbath-keeping; **Sadducees** regard **Eternal Life** as blasphemy

> **Ellis Rivkin** argues 1st century Jews did NOT persecute each other over religious differences, e.g. Pharisees & Sadducees coexisted despite being 'blasphemers'

(3) Threat to Power: Sadducees enjoyed great wealth and respect from managing the Temple; **Pharisees** respected as interpreters of the **Law**; **Romans** saw crowds as rioters and rebels

(4) Political Expedience: 'Expedience' = doing the practical thing even if you don't believe in it; **Romans** put down rebellion with great brutality; Jewish leaders protect their own people from these reprisals → arrest and execute innocent person to keep the peace (**Rivkin**)

- **Law of Moses:** contained in the Torah (Sadducees) plus later traditions (Pharisees)
- **Sabbath Controversies:** 'day of rest' established by God on 7th Day; 39 types of forbidden work (*MELAKHOT*); LEGALISTIC – putting laws before loving God/neighbours
- **Temple Cleansing:** massive complex with golden roofs and marble pillars; market and tourist trap; 'cleansing' = replacing it with a purer form of worship (**blasphemy** + **threat to the power** for Sadducees)

5.2 CONFLICT IN JOHN'S GOSPEL (Anthology #6)

JESUS CLEARS THE TEMPLE COURTS (John 2: 12-25)

Context: This takes place at start of Jesus' ministry (**John**) or before his arrest (Synoptics),

Jesus visits the Temple and is appalled at the commerce going on in the Outer Courts (moneychangers selling silver shekels to pay Temple Tax, merchants selling animals to be sacrificed); Jesus drives the sellers out with a whip, calls Temple a *market* (or *den of thieves* in **Matthew**)

Conflict: (1) calls God *Father*, claims authority of Son over Father's house; (2) insults a holy place, prevents sacrifices ordered in Torah; (3) threat to Sadducees' power/wealth; (4) riot/rebellion

Jerusalem is established as the locus of Jesus' sharpest conflict with unbelief which has been hardened by misunderstanding of the scriptures, institutions and festivals of Judaism – **R. Alan Culpepper**

Implications: Jesus refers to rebuilding Temple in 3 days = prediction of Resurrection BUT interpreted by his enemies as threatening to destroy Temple

At Jesus' trial (Synoptics), he is accused of claiming that he planned to destroy the Temple then rebuild it in three days; this is a distortion of what Jesus **actually** said but reflects his threat to power

AUTHORITY OF THE SON/TESTIMONIES ABOUT JESUS (John 5: 16-47)

Context: Link to Topic 2.3 (Miracles & Signs) Healing of the Blind Man; Jesus compares himself to John the Baptist

Jesus heals a man born blind by making clay from dust and spittle and pasting it on the man's eyes (breaking two rules: healing and making things); the Pharisees investigate by interrogating the man and his parents

Conflict: (1) calls God *my Father* and suggests he is co-creator, *equal with God*; (2) breaks Sabbath rules; (3) tells Pharisees the do not understand Scriptures, suggests Law does not give Eternal Life; (4) John the Baptist executed by Herod Antipas for troublemaking → this will happen to Jesus too

Implications: Jesus argues Jewish leaders have misunderstood the Scriptures and God; they are not the 'real' Judaism but a fake

The real conflict is not between Jesus and the Jews... but between Jesus and those who refuse to accept the revelation he brings. Unbelief is the real opponent – **R. Alan Culpepper**

DIVISIONS OVER WHO JESUS IS/UNBELIEF OF JEWISH LEADERS (John 7: 25-52)

Context: Feast of Tabernacles (Jewish harvest festival, Temple lit up at night); speaks about going back to God but this is mistaken for him leaving the country; enemies debate whether Jesus can be the Messiah since he is Galilean; soldiers fail to arrest Jesus

Conflict: (1) Going back to God = *Logos* who comes from God (*c.f.* **Topic 2.1 (Prologue in John)**), *"Where I am, you cannot come"* uses "I AM" formula (*c.f.* **Topic 2.2 (I Am Statements in John)**); (3) Pharisees losing their grip over people when their own soldiers disobey them

He was in the world, and though the world was made through him, the world did not recognize him – **John 1: 10**

Implications: divisions among Jews might reflect 1st century debates within Synagogues between Jewish Christians and their opponents; Matthew's birth-narrative/proof-texts (*c.f.* **Topic 1.1 (Prophecy Concerning the Messiah)**) addresses Jesus' origins; Jesus doesn't leave country but his teachings do spread among *the Greeks* (= Gentiles)

DISPUTES & JESUS' CLAIMS ABOUT HIMSELF (John 8: 12-59)

Context: Jesus has delivered **"I am the Light of the World"** (it is still Feast of Tabernacles at the illuminated Temple but Jesus is the true Temple); Jewish Law demands 2 witnesses to prove a statement so Jesus cites himself and God; Jesus claims Jewish leaders are children of the Devil

Conflict: (1) "I AM" statements (*c.f.* **Topic 2.2 (I Am Statements in John)**) = Light of the World + *before Abraham was, I am*, Jesus claims to speak *from the beginning* (= **Genesis**); (2) they try to stone Jesus for blasphemy; (3) Jewish leaders not children of Abraham and *do not belong to God*

One who blasphemes the name of the Lord shall be put to death – **Leviticus 24: 16**

Implications: Total failure of Jewish leaders to understand who Jesus is; he knows their Laws better than they do because he is the source of those laws; **Eternal Life** comes through believing in Jesus not obeying Law; reference to *Samaritans* may reflect Johannine Community's members

THE PHARISEES INVESTIGATE THE HEALING (John 9: 13-34)

Context: Link to Topic 2.3 (Miracles & Signs) Healing of the Blind Man: Pharisees interrogate the man born blind about who healed him on the Sabbath; they question his parents too

Conflict: (1) formerly-blind man regards Jesus as a prophet then later (**John 9: 38**, not in Anthology) as *Son of Man* and *Lord*; (2) confessing Jesus to be the Messiah seen as blasphemy, believers *put out of the Synagogue*; (3) growing disrespect towards the Pharisees (e.g. sarcasm)

Implications: Christology escalates → may reflect history of the Johannine Community; Christians banished from Synagogues reflects events c.90 CE (after Council of Jamnia, Jews rejected Christianity) → **Form Criticism** says this is *pericope* reflecting situations AFTER Jesus' ministry

FURTHER CONFLICT OVER JESUS' CLAIMS (John 10: 22-42)

Context: Festival of Hanukkah (midwinter, celebrating re-founding of Temple itself); Jesus declares he is one with God; he is forced to flee Jerusalem for the Jordan Valley

Conflict: (1) *"I and the Father are one"* = claim to be God; (2) *"you, a mere man, claim to be God"* = accusation of blasphemy

Implications: Return to Jordan brings Jesus 'full circle' to where John's Gospel started:

He came to that which was his own, but his own did not receive him – **John 1: 1**

Hanukkah celebrates miracle of God's light entering the world → refers to Jesus entering the world as **Light** (*c.f.* **Topic 2.1 (Prologue in John)**), not the physical Temple

The Jews legalistically maintain their observance of the festivals but <u>do not recognise the reality they celebrate</u> – **R. Alan Culpepper**

THE PLOT TO KILL JESUS (John 11: 45=57)

Context: Link to Topic 2.3 (Miracles & Signs) Raising Lazarus from the Dead: Caiaphas summons meeting of Sanhedrin to debate Jesus and persuades them to execute him

Conflict: (3) priests motivated by fear that *everyone will believe in him*; (4) execution justified by fear that *the Romans will come and take away both our temple and our nation*

Implications: statement that *one man dies for the people* describes Jesus' atoning death; suggests priests are religiously motivated (**Rivkin** rejects this) but hints at political expediency too

EVALUATING JESUS' CONFLICT WITH THE AUTHORITIES IN JOHN

Why it matters: All 4 Gospels describe this conflict but most intense in **John**; Judaism seen as legalistic, soulless and depraved → Christian antisemitism, persecution of Jews and the Holocaust; Jews were collectively blamed for DEICIDE (murdering God);

Conflict is...	Interpretation	Evaluation
Accurate	Jewish leaders had Jesus executed for blasphemy on false political charges	**Rivkin** argues Jews had live-and-let-live attitude and wouldn't do this
Exaggerated	Conflict really reflects arguments between 1st century Christians & Jews, not events in Jesus' ministry	Based on **Form Criticism** & **Redaction Criticism** – assumes Gospels not eyewitnesses
Distorted	Conflict was historical but Jews did not execute people for blasphemy (**Rivkin**)	**Paul** writes about being beaten and stoned for blasphemy in 40s-50s CE
Symbolic	Conflict is symbolic for faith vs *"the world's unbelief"* (**Culpepper**) – similar to **Parable of the Sower**	Also assumes Gospels not eyewitnesses and ignores Paul's experiences

5.2 JESUS' ARREST & TRIAL (Anthology #6 cont'd)

JESUS ARRESTED

Context: Judas has already agreed to betray Jesus; in Synoptics this happens on Passover night after a *seder* meal but **John** dates this as Passover Eve

After his final meal with his Disciples, Jesus spends the night in the Garden of Gethsemane on the Mount Olives. The Temple soldiers, guided by the traitor Judas, come to arrest him. Jesus goes peacefully, telling his Disciples not to use violence.

Conflict: (1) "I am" statement literally knocks guards over; (3) Jesus not intimidated by power of the Jewish leaders, goes willingly, forbids violence; (4) arrest by night is to prevent a crowd protesting and riots

Implications: Jesus affects guards as a **numinous religious experience**; he is always in total control (he goes to Judas, not *vice versa* as in Synoptics); reference to *drinking a cup* alludes to Jesus' prayer in Synoptics to be spared ordeal (which **John** omits but shows he knows about it); 'Malchus' (= 'king') refers to worldly rulers who really have no power (= Pilate, later on)

HIGH PRIEST QUESTIONS JESUS

Context: Unlike the Synoptics, John describes interrogation by former High Priest **Annas**; Jesus sent to High Priest **Caiaphas** but **John** does not describe this meeting (but Synoptics do)

Conflict: (3) Jesus questions the legitimacy of his arrest and is struck for it; (4) **John** presents the arrest as an abduction: illegal and violent (contrast with Jesus' peacefulness)

Ellis Rivkin argues the 'trial' really was a small, political plot involving just a few influential people, not a formal religious meeting; **John**'s account backs up Rivkin

Implications: Although they hide behind the appearance of legal process, the Jewish leaders act illegally: links to attitude to the **Law of Moses** which they claim to respect but do not understand;

PETER'S DENIALS

Context: Peter's denials feature in all four Gospels; **John** includes the 'Beloved Disciple' who gets access to the High Priest's house

Hiding outside the High Priest's house, Peter is approached by 3 servants who accuse him of being a Disciple; he denies it 3 times – just as Jesus predicted he would

Conflict: (1) "*I am not*" = reversal of Jesus' distinctive **"I Am" sayings**

Implications: passes CRITERION OF EMBARRASSMENT (Christians wouldn't invent a story that makes main leader look); contrast with Jesus' courage and frankness

JESUS BEFORE PILATE

Context: Pontius Pilate = governor (technically, *prefect*) of Judea since 26 CE; Jews become unclean if they enter a Gentile's house so Pilate comes to them outside; only the Romans have the legal right to execute prisoners

Pilate questions Jesus to see if he is a political rebel but decides he isn't; he offers to release a different prisoner but the crowd chooses **Barabbas** (a rebel who led an uprising)

Conflict: (1) Jesus admits to being a spiritual King *not of this world* not an earthly one; (3) if he claims to be 'King of the Jews' Jesus is a threat to Roman power, **Barabbas** is a real rebel who is a threat;

Implications: lots of irony (Jews want to remain clean but plot to kill Jesus, Pilate acknowledges Jesus is king, Roman law results in acquitting the guilty and condemning the innocent); Pilate represents the ordinary Roman citizen (or modern person) making their mind up about Jesus: is he crazy, a victim of circumstances or God?

It is [Pilate] who is on trial and his judgment will be a verdict on himself as much as it is on Jesus – **R. Alan Culpepper**

JESUS SENTENCED TO BE CRUCIFIED

Context: A crowd puts pressure on Pilate (who fears a riot); Jesus continues to be calm and does not respect the legitimacy of this trial at all

Pilate has Jesus whipped rather than execute him; the crowd threatens to complain to the Emperor if Pilate goes against their wishes; Pilate sentences Jesus to death by crucifixion – a punishment for rebels, outlaws and runaway slaves

Conflict: (1) Jesus is dressed as the King he truly is; (2) the priests want Jesus executed because *he claimed to be the Son of God*; (4) Pilate executes Jesus for fear of political repercussions, not because he thinks he's guilty

Implications: more irony (Jews want to remain clean but plot to kill Jesus, Pilate acknowledges Jesus is king, Jews deny God is their King, Pilate echoes *"Where do you come from?"* question); Jesus is politically innocent but condemned for religious reasons (**Rivkin** rejects this idea)

Rivkin argues Jesus was killed by "*the Roman imperial system*" with its "*cruelty and ruthless disregard for the human spirit*"; Jewish leaders were as much victims of this system as Jesus (so too, in his way, was Pilate).

EVALUATING THE TRIAL OF JESUS

Why it matters: addresses the question 'Who Killed Jesus?' – Romans or Jews? Blaming Jews resulted in centuries of Christian antisemitism; **Ellis Rivkin** argues for 'WHAT Killed Jesus?' and blames Roman politics which forced Jews to condemn fellow-Jews

Trial is...	Interpretation	Evaluation
Accurate	Jewish leaders pressured Pilate to convict Jesus of a political crime because of his blasphemy; Jews guilty of Jesus' death, Romans unwilling accomplices	**Rivkin** argues Jews had live-and-let-live attitude and wouldn't do this; Pilate was *stubborn and cruel*, not easily pushed around
Distorted	Jewish leaders and Pilate worked together to convict Jesus as a political threat to law & order (**Rivkin**'s view); Jews & Romans both guilty and both unwilling	1st century Christians wanted to present Jesus as respectable to the Roman Empire → shifted the blame onto Jews
Symbolic	Pilate symbolises "*the impossibility of compromise*" when it comes to judging who Jesus is (**R. Alan Culpepper**'s view); trial doesn't reflect historical Jews or Romans	Links to **Brown**'s view that John's Gospel was written for *crypto-Christians* afraid to 'come out' as believers

Evaluating Rivkin's view: Jesus killed by "*Roman imperial system*"

For: High Priest known to collaborate with Roman governors; Jesus attracted crowds and carried out provocative acts (e.g. cleansing the Temple); previous religious leaders had been executed for being politically dangerous (e.g. **John the Baptist**, according to **Josephus**); plausible that Disciples would not have understood politics going on and believed blasphemy was the crime

Against: Law of Moses sentences death for blasphemy; later Christian martyrs executed by High Priest for purely religious reasons (e.g. Stephen, James); **Paul** describes being beaten/stoned by Jews for religious reasons; Jewish population could (and did) complain to Emperor – Pilate later lost his job for ordering a massacre of Samaritans

Evaluating Culpepper's view: John's Gospel best read as literature

For: already lots of symbolism in **John's Gospel**; interpretation fits in with context in which Gospels were first read (readers would suffer costs if they converted to Christianity)

Against: trial is described similarly in Synoptic Gospels which are less symbolic; Pilate clearly a historical figure; trial passes CRITERION OF EMBARRASSMENT (Christians would not invent their founder being executed as a rebel) so probably historical not fictional

> **GOOD QUOTE** *[Pilate's] dilemma – to do the right thing or the popular thing – is every ruler's quandary. Perhaps that is why people can sympathise with him: we too must sometimes face a difficult choice* – **Kevin Butcher**

5.3 CRUCIFIXION & RESURRECTION IN LUKE (Anthology #7)

THE CRUCIFIXION OF JESUS

Context: Crucifixion = shameful for Romans and a curse for Jews:

> *anyone who is hung on a pole is under God's curse* – **Deuteronomy 21: 23**

Romans crucified in public; victim carries cross-bar to site; crowd encouraged to mock victims

> Jesus carries his cross to *Golgotha* (the 'place of the skull'); he makes a prophecy about the Apocalypse to the 'daughters of Jerusalem'; **Simon of Cyrene** is forced to carry Jesus' cross; soldiers divide up Jesus' clothes; Jesus is crucified between two thieves; the crowd mocks him but one thief asks Jesus for forgiveness

Forgiveness of Sins: Jesus prays to God to forgive his enemies → forgiveness of all human sins; thief repents his sins and Jesus assures him he is forgiven.

Future of the Church: Simon of Cyrene = Christian convert (his sons are in **Mark**) → Christianity spreads through compassion for Jesus' suffering, e.g. Thief admiring Jesus' goodness

Power of God: Jesus describes God acting in strength on future Day of Judgment (e.g. 'daughters of Jerusalem') AND God fulfils prophecies in Scriptures

> *A pack of villains encircles me; they pierce my hands and my feet* - **Psalm 22: 16 refers to crucifixion and thieves**
> *They divide my clothes among them and cast lots for my garment* – **Psalm 22: 18 refers to soldiers dividing Jesus' clothes**

God's *"veiled and secret"* power (**Marshall**) transforms lives and triggers repentance:

> Jesus mocked because he cannot *save himself*. **Frank Matera** calls this *"the paradox of the cross"* (*"whoever loses their life for me will save it"* – **Luke 9: 24**):
>
> "*Jesus is everything that the rulers, soldiers and criminal mockingly call him. But they do not understand the truth of their own speech since they cannot comprehend the paradox of the cross*" – **Frank J. Matera**

Sacrifice: Simon of Cyrene carrying Jesus' cross and following Jesus symbolises true discipleship:

> *Whoever wants to be my disciple must deny themselves and take up their cross daily and follow me* – **Luke 9: 23**

Salvation: Penitent Thief represents all humans in need of salvation: triggered by compassion for Jesus' suffering → feels guilt for his own sins, leading to confession + repentance → faith in Christ to save him: ideal model of Christian spirituality

THE DEATH OF JESUS

Context: death from crucifixion through blood loss and suffocation takes 1-3 days but much less if exhausted or legs broken (Jesus has been awake for 24 hours, beaten, whipped, too tired to carry cross – dies after 6 hours)

 Jesus was crucified at 9am; at 12pm the sun goes dark; at 3pm the veil in the Temple is torn in half, Jesus offers up his spirit to God and dies; Roman centurion admits that Jesus was blameless; crowds are sorry for what has happened; Jesus' female followers watch on

Forgiveness of Sins: torn Temple veil → **sacrifice** in the Temple is supposed to remove sins → Jesus is the true Temple/true sacrifice → sins are now forgiven; the crowd *beat their breasts* = showing guilt and repentance

Future of the Church: Centurion and crowd are moved by admiration for Jesus' innocent suffering; tearing of Temple veil symbolizes Gentiles now able to approach God

Power of God: darkness at noon shows God acting in strength (link to plagues in Egypt, also a reversal of God's first creative act to create light); admiration of Centurion & crowd shows *"veiled and secret"* power of God to spread compassion and love in place of hate

Sacrifice: Jesus is a perfect sacrifice; renders the Temple sacrifices redundant (=Temple veil torn)

Salvation: characters at different stages along this journey to salvation: the Centurion (compassion for Christ but does not repent), crowd (begun to repent but does not yet have faith)

THE BURIAL OF JESUS

Context: Romans leave crucified bodies to rot but Jewish Law forbids this, so Jesus taken down

 you must not leave the body hanging on the pole overnight. Be sure to bury it that same day – **Deuteronomy 21: 23**

Many rock tombs around the landscape of Jerusalem; women followers note which one Jesus is buried in (link to **Topic 6 (Challenges to the Resurrection)**).

 Jesus' body is taken down; a follower named Joseph of Arimathea provides a rock tomb; Jewish Law says a body must be treated with *spices and perfumes* but the Sabbath is about to begin (Friday sunset) so this must wait till Sunday morning

Future of the Church: new followers coming out of hiding (Joseph was secret sympathizer) → spread of Christianity in 1st century; detail of the *linen cloth* links to **Jesus Has Risen**

Power of God: *"veiled and secret"* power of God shown in concern for the corpse by Joseph and the women (and Pilate consenting to release the body)

Sacrifice: Jesus is placed in a king's tomb (cut out of rock, never used before)

Salvation: Joseph was *waiting for the Kingdom* and enters it when he reveals his loyalty to Jesus

THEORIES OF ATONEMENT

Moral Influence theory (MIT): Jesus' perfect life and forgiving death are inspiration → Thief repents, Centurion has compassion, crowd starts to repent → draws people into KoG; Luke's view and main theory for Early Church

Ransom theory: humans are property of the Devil because of sin; Jesus' **sacrifice** pays the 'ransom' → freeing humans from evil (link to Temple veil tearing since animal sacrifices ineffective, Jesus offering up his spirit); the other main theory of Early Church

Satisfaction theory: human sins offend God's goodness → Jesus' perfect suffering and death satisfies God's justice (link to Jesus forgiving enemies, offering up spirit); proposed by **Anselm** (1098 CE – same Anselm as **ontological argument**)

Penal Substitution theory: humans deserve punishment for sin but Jesus takes the punishment for us (link to Temple veil tearing) → no need for further sacrifices); popular Protestant theory

JESUS HAS RISEN

Context: women come to the tomb to prepare Jesus' body for burial by washing it and treating it with *spices and perfumes* as commanded by Jewish Law; this is Sunday, the first day of the Jewish week (*c.f.* **Topic 6.1 (Challenges to the Resurrection)**)

The rock tomb is open and empty; two strange men appear and announce that Jesus has risen, as he predicted back in Galilee; the women go to tell the Eleven; Peter goes to the tomb and finds only the linen grave cloth Jesus had been wrapped in

Future of the Church: Peter is future leader of the church; Luke later reveals Peter encounters Risen Jesus (but doesn't describe it); this view supported by **Paul** but other traditions make women (especially **Mary Magdalene**) first witnesses to Resurrection

Fulfillment of Scripture: Angels confirm Jesus as 'Son of Man' (cosmic judge from prophecy of Daniel); remind women that Jesus predicted this:

The Son of Man must suffer many things and be rejected by the elders, the chief priests and the teachers of the law, and he must be killed and on the third day be raised to life – **Luke 9: 22**

God's Saving Plan: the angels say "The Son of Man must be delivered..." → everything has happened according to God's plan

Power of God: God conquers death (introduced to world by sin of Adam & Eve – **Genesis 3: 19**)

By raising Jesus from the dead, God asserted his power in a definitive way over every malevolent power, whether on earth or in heaven – **Frank J. Matera**

Relationship with God: women are frightened (**numinous experience**) but understanding Jesus' words changes this; Disciples do not believe them because they do not yet understand Jesus; even Peter does not yet believe (evidence alone is insufficient without teachings of Scripture)

ON THE ROAD TO EMMAUS

Context: Same Sunday morning; Cleopas might by *Clopas the husband of Mary* (who was at Crucifixion) → other Disciple might be wife Mary; Cleopas = 'procaimer' so symbolic → other disciple = reader (Luke uses 'disciple' to mean any follower of Christ, not just the Twelve)

Two disciples of Jesus walk from Jerusalem to Emmaus; they meet Jesus but do not recognise him; they discuss their disappointment and the empty tomb but Jesus *opens* Scripture to them; they invite Jesus to eat with them; when he breaks bread they recognise him then he disappears; they go back to Jerusalem to tell the Eleven

Future of the Church: these Disciples symbolise the Church = frightened, fleeing, confused → confident, gathering together, reinterpreting Scripture in light of Resurrection; Peter confirmed as first witness; women only saw *visions of angels* (is Luke demoting women's testimony? Or making case for Resurrection stronger by 1st century standards by not depending on females?)

Fulfilment of Scripture: Jesus shows how Old Testament predicts Resurrection (probably **Isaiah**'s **Suffering Servant, Psalm 22**); Jews treat these as referring to Israel personified

you will not abandon me to the realm of the dead,
nor will you let your faithful one see decay – **Psalm 16: 10**

Power of God: *"veiled and secret"* but revealed through sharing and Eucharist

Relationship with God: Jesus is encountered **mystically** in the **Eucharist** (= breaking bread)

JESUS APPEARS TO THE DISCIPLES

Context: Appearance to the Eleven is in all Gospels; Risen Jesus eating/being touched also in **John**

Jesus appears to the Eleven; they think he's a ghost so he eats fish and lets them touch him; he *opens their minds* to the true meaning of Scripture; tells them to preach to *all the nations* and promises them *power from on high*

Future of the Church: *all the nations* = making Gentile converts; *power from on high* = arrival of Holy Spirit at Pentecost (**Acts 2: 1-4**) → Luke's version of 'Great Commission' in **Matthew 28: 16**

Fulfillment of Scripture: *Moses* = the Torah (**Sadducees**); *the Prophets & the Psalms* = the Oral Law (**Pharisees**) → true meaning behind both Jewish sects

Power of God: Jesus is not a ghost; he has defeated death, not merely 'survived' it → a new mode of existence

He now enjoys a bodily existence that transcends the corporeal existence with which human beings are familiar – **Frank J. Matera**

Relationship with God: eyewitnesses do not automatically believe → correct understanding of Scripture leads to faith in Resurrection (important for future Christians after the Ascension)

THE ASCENSION OF JESUS

Context: the same day (but Acts 1: 9-11 says 40 days later) Bethany is home of Mary, Martha & Lazarus, just outside Jerusalem (Jesus' 'base' during his ministry in Judea)

Jesus leaves this world and enters a heavenly mode of existence; Luke describes this as rising upwards (quite literally in **Acts 1: 9-11**); Disciples return to Jerusalem to worship at Temple (but in **Acts** version, angels appear to send them to preach)

Future of the Church: Resurrection-appearances ceased → belief that Jesus had 'moved on' to rule from Heaven, replaced on Earth by his Holy Spirit until *Parousia* (delayed, according to Luke)

Fulfilment of Scripture: Isaiah's Suffering Servant and Daniel's Son of Man both enter the presence of God to be rewarded for their faithfulness = Jesus ascending to Heaven

God's Saving Plan: Jesus will return = *Parousia*, the 'Second Coming'; his departure is temporary while the Holy Spirit carries out his work on Earth through the Church

Relationship with God: Jesus' Ascension is beginning of God's plan to redeem the human race

Frank J. Matera calls the Resurrection *"a new creation animated and empowered by God's Spirit"* – not just one person being raised from the dead but the first stage in God's project to create the entire universe all over again, one person at a time

EVALUATING THE RESURRECTION

Why it matters: did Jesus return to physical life or did he return as a spirit? Or is the whole story symbolic for the triumph of good over evil, hope over despair, love over hate? Gospels (especially **Luke** and **John**) go out of their way to demonstrate a physical Resurrection

Resurrection is...	Interpretation	Evaluation
Physical	Jesus returned as a physical being; not his old body but a resurrected body that does not obey the laws of nature as we know them; not always recognisable even to friends; can be touched	Links to empty tomb and Disciples touching Jesus; does not explain spiritual encounter on road to Emmaus
Spiritual	Jesus returned as a spirit; could be seen and might seem physical; left his old body in the tomb; can appear in any form or disappear; not solid	Does not explain empty tomb; why would spirit fool people into thinking it was physical?
Symbolic	Jesus remained dead but 'rose again' in the hearts of his followers (**Bultmann**); his beliefs lived on and grew in power; they outlived Jerusalem Temple (fell in 70 CE) and Roman Empire (476 CE)	Does not explain why Disciples preached Resurrection as historical fact rather than a myth; does not explain empty tomb

TOPIC 5 EXAM QUESTIONS & REVISION ACTIVITIES

A-Level Paper 3 (New Testament)

Section A

1. Explore the religious conflicts in the ministry of Jesus in John's Gospel. (8 marks)

2. Assess the significance of the resurrection of Jesus for believers. (12 marks)

Section B

Read the following passage before answering the questions.

> [32] Two other men, both criminals, were also led out with him to be executed. [33] When they came to the place called the Skull, they crucified him there, along with the criminals – one on his right, the other on his left. [34] Jesus said, "Father, forgive them, for they do not know what they are doing." And they divided up his clothes by casting lots.
>
> [35] The people stood watching, and the rulers even sneered at him. They said, "He saved others; let him save himself if he is God's Messiah, the Chosen One."
>
> [36] The soldiers also came up and mocked him. They offered him wine vinegar [37] and said, "If you are the king of the Jews, save yourself."
>
> [38] There was a written notice above him, which read: THIS IS THE KING OF THE JEWS.
>
> [39] One of the criminals who hung there hurled insults at him: "Aren't you the Messiah? Save yourself and us!"
>
> [40] But the other criminal rebuked him. "Don't you fear God," he said, "since you are under the same sentence? [41] We are punished justly, for we are getting what our deeds deserve. But this man has done nothing wrong."
>
> [42] Then he said, "Jesus, remember me when you come into your kingdom."
>
> [43] Jesus answered him, "Truly I tell you, today you will be with me in paradise."
>
> Quote from New International Translation, Luke 23: 32-43

3. (a) Clarify the ideas illustrated in this passage about the significance of the Crucifixion. *You must refer to the passage in your response.* (10 marks)

   (b) Assess the claim that Jesus was "a *failed messiah*". (20 marks)

Section C

4. "The Kingdom of God will come about in the future."

   Evaluate this view in the context of differing views on the arrival of the Kingdom of God. In your response to this question, you must include how developments in New Testament Studies have been influenced by one of the following:

   - Philosophy of Religion
   - Religion and Ethics
   - the study of a religion.

   (30 marks)

   Total = 90 marks

In these example papers, all the questions are drawn from Topic 5. A real exam would not be like this and each question would probably draw from a different Topic instead..

Comprehension Quiz

1. What is meant by Kingdom of God?
2. What is the difference between a futurist and preterist understand of the Kingdom of God?
3. What is eschatology?
4. Give an example of an apocalyptic parable.
5. What was the cleansing of the Temple and why was it necessary?
6. Describe examples of Jesus doing or saying two things that would have been considered blasphemous by Jews of the 1st century.
7. Where does Ellis Rivkin lay the blame for Jesus' death?
8. Outline three reasons why Jesus had to die.
9. Why does Albert Schweitzer call Jesus a *"failed messiah"*?
10. In what way is Rudolf Bultmann 'rescuing' liberal theology?
11. Who was Pontius Pilate and what was his relationship with Caiaphas?
12. Give an example of Jesus' death fulfilling the Scriptures.
13. How does Jesus' death illustrate the moral influence theory of atonement?
14. What happened on the road to Emmaus?
15. What is the Ascension?

Bible Quotes to match

Explain how each quote links to this Topic

1. *you will not abandon me to the realm of the dead,
   nor will you let your faithful one see decay* – **Psalm 16: 10**

2. *"The coming of the kingdom of God is not something that can be observed, nor will people say, 'Here it is,' or 'There it is,' because the kingdom of God is in your midst"* – **Luke 17: 20-22**

3. *"Whoever wants to be my disciple must deny themselves and take up their cross daily and follow me"* – **Luke 9: 23**

4. *One who blasphemes the name of the Lord shall be put to death* – **Leviticus 24: 16**

5. *you must not leave the body hanging on the pole overnight. Be sure to bury it that same day* – **Deuteronomy 21: 23**

6. *He came to that which was his own, but his own did not receive him* – **John 1: 1**

7. *"whoever loses their life for me will save it"* – **Luke 9: 24**

A-Level Year 2 New Testament Studies

Word Search

Find 20 terms/names from this Topic and explain them

```
U R C O S N A P A Z T T Y A F
L E R O W O M R V B E O H J A
E W U W C I S I I M R T M S W
B O C X E T C A P M O A C B E
N S I H T C S L H G A E H S C
S M F I S E E U L P N T P A S
A A Y G P R C O A S A Y H A M
B G U C J R G J I M L I N E O
B D J B Z U Y O P A M I A G A
A A Z N N S N V C M M E I C F
R L O D F E O O K I N G D O M
A E W J D R P E T A L I P W Y
B N M B R A B E E L Z E B U B
C E T S I R A H C U E K R C G
J U D A S Z V Y X S W O C F I
```

Crossword

Across
2. Worth about 50 shekels
5. Prophet who preached a warning to Nineveh
7. They cannot go through the Eye of a Needle
9. Jesus accused people of turning Temple into this
10. _____-history, God's plan taking place over time
11. End of the world
13. Story with a spiritual meaning
14. God's rule over humanity

Down
1. He argues Jesus did not die for blasphemy
3. They represent worldly concerns in the Parable of the Sower
4. Simon of _____ carried Jesus' cross
5. _____ of Arimathea buried Jesus
6. Another name for the Devil
7. He suggests Luke reduced apocalyptic tone of Jesus
8. Argues against Conzelmann
10. Regards Jesus as a 'failed messiah'
12. City destroyed by God

Debates in this Topic

Indicate where you stand on this debate by marking a cross on the line then list points in favour and points against your position (more in favour the closer to the edge, more against the closer to the middle)

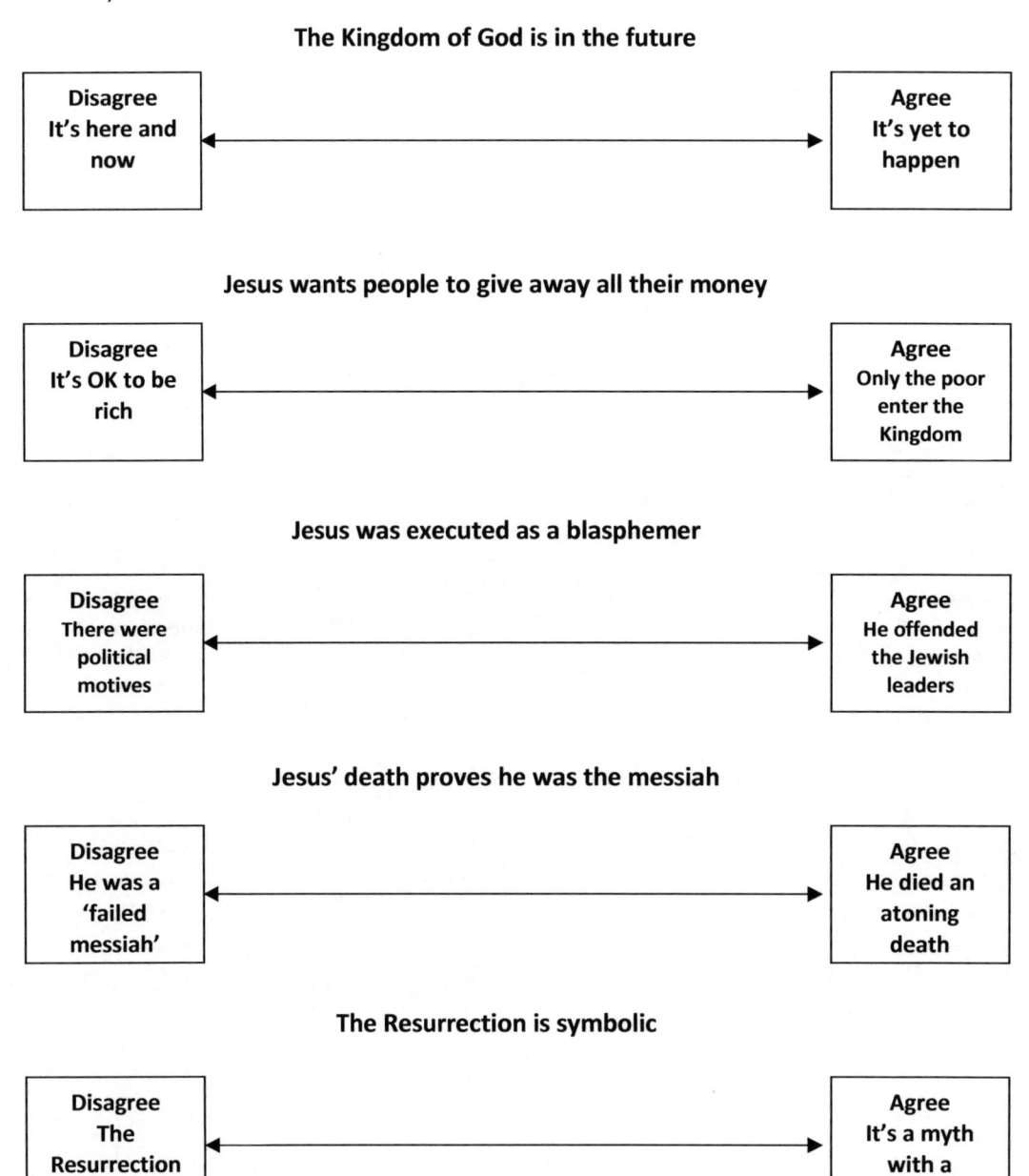

The Kingdom of God is in the future

| Disagree — It's here and now | ←————————→ | Agree — It's yet to happen |

Jesus wants people to give away all their money

| Disagree — It's OK to be rich | ←————————→ | Agree — Only the poor enter the Kingdom |

Jesus was executed as a blasphemer

| Disagree — There were political motives | ←————————→ | Agree — He offended the Jewish leaders |

Jesus' death proves he was the messiah

| Disagree — He was a 'failed messiah' | ←————————→ | Agree — He died an atoning death |

The Resurrection is symbolic

| Disagree — The Resurrection is historical | ←————————→ | Agree — It's a myth with a meaning |

Cloze Exercise

Jesus preached about the arrival of God's _____ on Earth, which he called the Kingdom of God. _____ argues that Jesus believed the arrival of the Kingdom to be imminent and that his crucifixion would trigger the Apocalypse. When this didn't happen, Jesus died a disappointed man and a "_____ messiah".

The first Christians expected the Kingdom to arrive when Jesus returned, an event called the _____ and which they expected would happen soon. _____ argues that, when it became clear this return was delayed, Christians came up with a new concept he calls _____-history. This is the idea that the Kingdom is in the future and first the church must grow on Earth, working through 'the _____' of history. He argues that distinctive features in _____'s Gospel illustrate this shift in thinking from _____ teachings to more long-term concerns like social justice and moral living.

_____ argues that early Christians all expected the apocalypse to be imminent but it was fulfilled by the destruction of _____ by the Romans in 70 CE.

Jesus' conflict with the authorities is explored in _____'s Gospel. Jesus is arrested and taken to _____ to be questioned, where he is slapped. _____ denies Jesus three times but Jesus is not intimidated. He tells the Roman governor that his kingdom is not of this _____. _____ does not want to execute Jesus but is frightened of the mob outside. First he releases a rebel called _____ then he whips Jesus but eventually he sentences him to be crucified.

Jesus carries his cross to the place of execution. When he is too exhausted, _____ carries it for him. Jesus is crucified between two _____, one of whom insults him but the other asks for forgiveness. Jesus promises the man will join him in _____.

Jesus _____ his enemies and commends his spirit to God before dying. The crowd beat their _____ which shows guilt. This illustrates the moral influence theory of _____, because Jesus' death triggers _____ in other people.

Jesus is buried straight away in a rock tomb so as not to break the law in _____ about leaving a corpse on a pole overnight. After the _____, the women come to prepare his body with _____ but find the tomb open and empty.

Disciples start having encounters with the Risen Jesus, including two on the road to _____ who do not recognise Jesus at first. Jesus eats _____ and allows himself to be touched to show he is not a _____. He then _____ into Heaven. His followers interpret the Scriptures in a radical new way as predicting Jesus' suffering and death. They believe his Resurrection is the beginning of God's _____ for humanity.

Annas, apocalyptic, ascends, atonement, Barabbas, chests, Conzelmann, Deuteronomy, Emmaus, failed, fish, forgives, ghost, Jerusalem, John, long haul, Luke, Marshall, Paradise, *Parousia*, Peter, Pontius Pilate, repentance, rule, Sabbath, salvation, saving plan, Schweitzer, Simon of Cyrene, spices & perfumes, thieves, world

6 SCIENTIFIC & HISTORICAL-CRITICAL CHALLENGES / ETHICAL LIVING

6.1 SCIENTIFIC & HISTORICAL-CRITICAL CHALLENGES

This topic looks at the death and resurrection of Jesus in modern scholarship, including **Enlightenment challenges** to the resurrection as a miracle and views of it as a **fiction**, a **myth** or a **subjective experience**. There are no key scholars but **Frank Morison** and **Ian Wilson** feature in the Anthology.

6.2 HOW SHOULD WE LIVE?

This topic covers Jesus' **sermon on the plain** in Luke's Gospel and 3 Parables (**Good Samaritan, Lost Sheep//Coin/Son** and **Rich Man & Lazarus**) as well as Jesus' teachings in **relation to Judaism**. Key scholars are **I. Howard Marshall** and (*we suppose*) **Frank J. Matera**.

KEY TERMINOLOGY:

Beatitudes: Blessings; Jesus pronounces blessings on the poor, the hungry, the weeping and the hated as part of the **Sermon on the Plain**

Empty Tomb: Phenomenon reported in all four Gospels that Jesus' tomb was discovered to be empty on Sunday morning

Hallucination Theory: Hypothesis that Jesus truly died but his disciples hallucinated his Resurrection appearances (a subjective experience)

Myth: A story which is not historically true but which contains a meaningful message or idea

Samaritan: Community of Palestinian people hated by 1st century Jews but preserving their own religious traditions about God, Moses and the Messiah

Sermon on the Plain: Ethical teaching in Luke 6, consisting of 4 blessings (**beatitudes**), 4 woes, love your enemy, golden rule and parables about hypocrisy

Substitute Theory: Hypothesis that the person who died on the cross was not Jesus but a double, perhaps his twin; real Jesus mistaken by Disciples for having come back from dead

Swoon Theory: Hypothesis that Jesus passed out on the cross but did not die; he revived in the tomb and was released by friends (possibly **Essenes**); Disciples mistook this for a miracle

Theft Theory: Hypothesis that Jesus' corpse was stolen from the tomb (by his disciples or perhaps by the authorities); linked to idea Resurrection is a hoax or a mistake

Vision Theory: Hypothesis that Jesus died but God sent visions of Jesus to communicate with his disciples (not a subjective experience)

6.1 CHALLENGES TO THE RESURRECTION

THE RESURRECTION AS A MIRACLE

Resurrection goes against laws of nature (dead do not come back to life)

Implications: Deists reject interventionist God; God does not go against own (scientific) laws:

> **GOOD QUOTE**: *miracles contradict the order of creation* – **Hermann Reimarus**

Criticism: if interventionist God of Bible is real, then *order of creation* is **supposed** to be contradicted, e.g. Resurrection

EXAMPLE: David Hume (1748): Scottish philosopher, sceptic, wrote *On Miracles*; argues rational person never believes in miracles because other explanations *always* more probable

> **GOOD QUOTE**: *it is a miracle, that a dead man should come to life; because that has never been observed in any age or country* – **David Hume**

Implications: people believe miracles like Resurrection because they enjoy feeling *surprise and wonder* (link to **Form Criticism: Debelius** identifies 'tales'), especially *ignorant and barbarous nations* without scientific progress; may lie about miracles to *promote a holy cause*

Criticism: Hume's argument is CIRCULAR (assumes miracles never happen → accounts of miracle unlikely to be true); people in 1st century weren't THAT gullible (reactions of disbelief in Gospels)

> **GOOD QUOTE**: *The discovery that dead people stay dead was not first made by the philosophers of the Enlightenment* – **N.T. Wright**

THE RESURRECTION AS A FICTION

Naturalistic (non-supernatural) explanation = "Theft Hypothesis": disciples stole Jesus' corpse → faked the Resurrection (perhaps unintentionally: women at tomb may have misunderstood)

Implications: e.g. Matthew 28: 11-15 (Jewish priests bribe guards to say disciples stole corpse)

Criticism: disciples would not embrace persecution and death for a lie; someone would talk

EXAMPLE: Karl Friedrich Barhdt (1741-1792): "Swoon Hypothesis": Jesus did not die on cross → recovery mistaken for Resurrection

Implications: supported by only 6 hours to die (short time); Barhdt proposes conspiracy to rescue Jesus from tomb (men in white robes = **Essenes** mistaken for angels by women)

Criticisms: Not short time to die since Jesus beaten and whipped during trial, couldn't carry own cross = exhausted; executioners knew what they were doing; traumatic wounds → could not convince anyone he had risen from the dead in such a condition

> **GOOD QUOTE**: *half-dead out of the sepulchre ... weak and ill, wanting medical treatment ... [would not look like] a Conqueror over death and the grave, the Prince of life* – **David Strauss**

THE RESURRECTION AS A MYTH

1st century beliefs about pagan gods/Jewish prophets got 'attached' to story of Jesus; 'Mythicist Theory' = Jewish/pagan converts added myths to story of Jesus

Examples: Anthropologists find DYING-AND-RISING GOD in most cultures; JEWISH = **Suffering Servant** in **Isaiah:** dies then returns to life; **Elijah:** immortal, will return to Earth one day; **PAGAN = Osiris:** birth heralded by a star, healer, betrayed & murdered, body hidden → returned from dead, reigns in heaven, judges the dead

Implications: Christians originally believed in SPIRITUAL RESURRECTION (e.g. Paul's vision of Christ) → myth took over that Jesus had returned to physical life; link to Rudolf Bultmann (mythological world view vs scientific world view)

Criticism: story of Jesus does not resemble a myth because specific dates (Resurrection on April 23, 33 CE) and places (Jerusalem) not "once upon a time"; earliest Christians = Jews, believed in physical Afterlife, later converts = Gentiles, believed in spiritual Afterlife, so wrong way round

EXAMPLE: David Strauss (1835): refuted "Theft" & "Swoon" Hypotheses; disciples attributed to Jesus myths about Jewish Messiah; myths = *"ideas formulated in unintentionally poeticizing sagas and looking very like history"* – **David Strauss**

Implications: there is spiritual truth in myths (not *false*) but not *history*i; express feelings that are important to believers = love for Jesus never died; disciples not lying or deceiving, just deluded

Criticism: Jesus does *not* fit Jewish **Messiah** (e.g. from Galilee), **Suffering Servant** (e.g. it represents Israel) or **son of David** (e.g. problems with genealogy); Resurrection → first New Testament texts = 30 years, not long enough for myth-making

THE RESURRECTION AS A SUBJECTIVE EXPERIENCE

Resurrection sightings = hallucinations or visions; **David Strauss** (1835) argues disciples *"incapable of thinking of Jesus as dead"* → *"deluded into thinking that he had risen"*

Implications: disciples were hysterical (perhaps first Mary Magdalene → Peter → other disciples); brought on by stress (persecution) + guilt (abandoning Jesus); they imagined what they most wished for

Criticism: rejected in 2nd century by **Origen** → disciples *"neither mentally unbalanced nor delirious"*; disciples preached in the streets, wrote epistles (letters) → no sign of mental illness

EXAMPLE: Jack Kent (1999): *"normal, grief-related hallucinations"* explain Resurrection sightings; not uncommon for healthy people to hallucinate seeing dead loved ones

Implications: **Peter** = guilt over denying Jesus; **Paul** = inner conflict over persecution of Christians → *"conversion disorder"*; temporary psychotic (hallucinating) symptom in healthy person

Criticism: people in 1st century familiar with grief and hysteria (e.g. they do not believe the women at first); disciples doubt their own eyes → they touch Jesus and speak with him as a group → an OBJECTIVE experience; **Paul** writes if Jesus did not rise from the dead *"our preaching is useless and so is your faith"* so LIFELONG CONVICTION not temporary delusion

6.1 FRANK MORISON (Anthology #8)

Frank Morison (1881-1950): journalist, intended to expose Resurrection as a 'myth' → concluded it was historical fact instead: *"it effected a revolution in my thought"* – **Frank Morison**

Why was tomb empty?	Morison's comments	Evaluation
Disciples stole the body (Theft Hypothesis)	Early Church was *"great moral structure"* based on *"lifelong persecution & personal suffering"* → couldn't be based on known lie	Might be idealizing disciples too much (e.g. **Hume** says fanatics lie for *holy causes*); thieves might be rival group of disciples (e.g. **Essenes**) who didn't join Church (wiped out by Romans in 70 CE)
Joseph of Arimathea removed the body	Makes no sense to do this at night; would not have kept it secret; no rumours about alternative tomb for Jesus	Shallow Grave hypothesis = Jesus never buried at all (Romans dispose of corpses in shallow grave), entire tomb story is fictional
Authorities removed the body	Pilate was *"very obstinate man"* → would not change his mind; authorities placed guards to PREVENT removal; authorities could produce the body later but didn't	Ascension was 40 days after Resurrection → corpse would be 7 weeks old when Christians preaching = unrecognisable; also, authorities must admit what they did (this makes them look sinful or frightened)
Jesus did not die (Swoon Theory)	Theory *"ignores deadly character of the wounds"*; considers **David Strauss** (1865) the *"death blow"* to this theory	Does not take into account conspiracy (e.g. **Essenes**) to open tomb, remove grave cloth, provide medical help; however, most scholars agree with Morison
Women made a mistake	Criticises theory of **Kirsopp Lake** (1907): depends on disciples being in Galilee but why would they abandon their female friends & family?	There DO seem to be different contenders for the Tomb; however, women's mistake could have been quickly corrected so most scholars agree with Morison
Women never visited tomb	Christians could not preach Resurrection if Jesus' body was still in nearby tomb that was easily visited	Ignores possibility first Christians preached SPIRITUAL RESURRECTION (body irrelevant) → tomb lost in 70 CE when Romans invade → later Christians shift to belief in physical Resurrection

Criticisms: Morison is CHERRY-PICKING: harmonises Gospels into one narrative, ignoring details that don't support him (e.g. **Matthew 28: 2**, women see angel open the tomb); ignores **Hume**'s idea = even improbable naturalistic explanations (e.g. visiting wrong tomb) more likely than miracles

6.1 IAN WILSON (Anthology #9)

Ian Wilson (b. 1941): writer, sceptic who converted to (Catholic) Christianity, wrote book for TV documentary, tries to be balanced

Site of the tomb: Church of the Holy Sepulchre (CoHS) in Jerusalem = pagan temple, tomb re-discovered by Empress **Helena** in 4th century CE; 60 other rock tombs in Jerusalem; alternative = 'Garden Tomb'; Gospels describe tomb *outside* city walls → CoHS is *inside* walls BUT would have been outside 1st century Jerusalem → Helena didn't know that so her tradition may be genuine

> **Ian Wilson** rejects earthquake/angel in **Matthew** as *"pious embroideries by an author demonstrably over-fond of the miraculous"* but suggests *"there remains no uncontested rational answer"* to *"the central mystery of the Christian religion"* which is, How did this belief in the Resurrection come about?

Discrepancies between the Gospel accounts of the Resurrection:			
Matthew	**Mark**	**Luke**	**John**
Mary Magdalene is with another Mary	Mary Magdalene is with another Mary and Salome	Mary Magdalene is with another Mary and Joanna	Mary Magdalene arrives alone
An angel opens the tomb	The tomb is open and a young man is inside	The tomb is open and two men/angels appear	The tomb is open is empty
Jesus appears in Galilee	Jesus appears in Galilee	Jesus appears in Jerusalem	Jesus appears in Jerusalem

> **Ian Wilson** says accounts have *"the same quality as the memories of witnesses after a road accident"* → sounds like *"personal and highly confused versions of the same story"*; if invented, why **make women prime witnesses?** → *"women's testimony carried a particularly low weight in Jewish Law"*

6 possible hypotheses for the Resurrection:			
Hypothesis	**Comments**	**Hypothesis**	**Comments**
1. Women went to wrong tomb	*"an easy matter for any sceptic to … set the whole matter at rest"*	2. Someone removed body	*"we might surely have expected someone, some time, to produce it"*
3. Disciples stole body	Thief would confess under persecution	4. Hallucination	Does not explain Empty Tomb
5. Jesus survived crucifixion	**Strauss:** *"a being who had stolen half dead out of the sepulchre"* nothing like *"the Prince of Life"*	6. Jesus rose from the dead	Change in *"previously denying and demoralized"* disciples → *"something like [Resurrection] actually happened."*

3.2 THE SERMON ON THE PLAIN

Similar to 'Sermon on the Mount' in **Matthew**; from the **Q-source**; same sermon or different one with similar themes? Luke's 'Sermon on the Plain' (SoP) aimed at Gentiles as well as Jews

> **Frank J. Matera** argues Matthew's Sermon *"to show that Jesus did not come to abolish the Law and the Prophets but to fulfil them"* → Luke's "SoP" *"focuses on the need to extend love to all, even to one's enemy"*

THE BLESSINGS (BEATITUDES) & WOES

Blessed are... (Beatitudes)	Consequence	Woe to	Consequence
those who are **POOR**	Enter Kingdom of God (KoG): *c.f.* thorns in **Parable of Sower (PoS)**	those who are **RICH**	You already received comfort: afterlife *c.f.* **Rich Man & Lazarus**
those who are **HUNGRY** now	Satisfied : eschatological (future KoG or afterlife); Jesus is **Bread of Life**	those who are **WELL-FED** now	Hungry: Hell in afterlife or lack of spiritual nourishment in this life?
those who **WEEP** now	Laugh: eschatological (KoG = party) *c.f.* **Sign of Water into Wine, Parable of Great Banquet**	those who **LAUGH** now	Mourn and weep: reference to mocking crowds at Crucifixion
those who are **HATED** for the sake of the Son of Man	You are like prophets the Jews rejected: criticism of Judaism, *c.f.* **PoS**, good seed *perseveres*	YOU, if everyone **SPEAKS WELL** of you	You are like false prophets: Christianity isn't supposed to make you popular/successful

1st century Judaism: very Jewish tone; **Psalm 41** blesses those who help the poor, **Psalm 107** promises God will *fill the hungry soul*, **Isaiah 61: 2** promises God will comfort those who mourn; however, condemns **Pharisees/Sadducees** as rejecting true prophets

Christian codes of living: give to the poor, feed the hungry, comfort the unhappy and to bear suffering and persecution cheerfully e.g. **Francis of Assisi** gave up all his possessions, entirely dependent on God for food and shelter, joyful despite painful illness; condemning 'Laughers' links to Christian censorship of satire and criticism

Equality today: 'pie in the sky' consolation for putting up with injustice vs 'call to arms' to challenge inequality of wealth and opportunity; Western societies are collectively *well-fed* compared to developing countries

Pluralism today: In 2016, **Pope Francis** offered 6 new Beatitudes to *"recognise and respond to new situations with fresh energy"* e.g. support abandoned/marginalized, care for environment → blessings cover people who aren't necessarily Christian

LOVE YOUR ENEMIES + GOLDEN RULE

> *love your enemies, do good to those who hate you* – **Luke 6: 27**

Illustrations: slapped = *turn the other cheek*; coat taken = *give shirt too*; don't ask for something back if someone takes it; Jesus is slapped at his trial; guards divide his clothes → forgives his enemies from the cross; love = *agape* (selfless, compassionate love: a choice not a feeling)

Implications: beyond 'law of reciprocity' (treat others the way they treat you) → altruism: treat others well *regardless* of how they treat you; unrealistic 'counsel of perfection'?

> *Do to others as you would have them do to you* – **Luke 6: 31**

Implications: beyond 'law of reciprocity' → treat others the way you'd *like* to be treated

1st century Judaism: focus on law of reciprocity ("*eye for an eye*" in **Leviticus 24: 20** = *lex talionis*/law of retaliation) vs Jewish teacher **Hillel the Elder** (110 BCE – 10 CE) summed up Torah as: "*What is hateful to you, do not do to your fellow.*"

Christian codes of living: APOCALYPTICISTS believed in imminent end of the world → demanding ethical rules followed for a short time; '*Parousia* Delay' → less extreme ethical code, e.g. 'Just War' Theory; link to PASSIVE RESISTANCE (**Gandhi, Martin Luther King**) in 20th century

Equality today: Golden Rule = treat others as equals (*especially* if they are enemies)

Pluralism today: Golden Rule supports religious liberty (freedom to practise your religion) + religious toleration (duty to put up with other religions); debates about faith schools, religious dress codes and extremist violence

'DO NOT JUDGE' + TEACHINGS ABOUT HYPOCRISY

Hypocrisy = 'saying one thing but doing the opposite'; warns against '**judging**' other people (condemning them for their faults); merciful/forgiving → God will be merciful/forgive you

> *Human judgement is flawed because it cannot fully understand the heart and motives of the other. Moreover, those who judge others rarely understand their own motives and faults* – **Frank J. Matera**

- **The Blind Leading the Blind:** *they both fall into a pit*; so-called guide pretending to be wiser than he really is
- **The Log in the Eye:** friend has *speck of sawdust* in eye (= minor fault) vs *plank* in your own eye; critic more guilty than person they are criticizing
- **Fruit Tree & its Fruit:** different types of fruit trees = different types of people; *figs/grapes* = good; *thornbushes/briers* = sinners; 'actions speak louder than words'; link to Fig Tree = Jewish nation; Vine = Judaism but Jesus is **True Vine** (*c.f.* **"I Am" statements in John**)
- **Wise & Foolish Builders:** teachings = rock foundations: things built on them will last; link to **Beelzebub** invading strong man's house (*c.f.* **Kingdom of God in Luke**)

1st century Judaism: Judaism largely external (sacrifices, washing, foods, Sabbath regulations) → easy to judge a 'good Jew': a person can still have evil thoughts, be selfish; Jesus focuses on positive altruism → development on Jewish ethics

Christian codes of living: potential for Christian hypocrisy after 4th century CE Christianity became official religion of Roman Empire; **Existentialism** values authenticity, **Rudolf Bultmann** de-mythologizes Christianity to make message more accessible

Equality today: discrimination starts with judging other groups harshly (prejudice); *'love the sinner, hate the sin'* (**Augustine of Hippo**) = judge BEHAVIOUR but love/respect PERSON

Pluralism today: religious liberty + religious tolerance based on not judging other religions

EVALUATING THE SERMON ON THE PLAIN

Matera's view that SoP offers practical ethics for living

For: Jesus intended his ethics to be followed as rules, not vague ideals

> *Why do you call me, 'Lord, Lord,' and do not do what I say?* – **Luke 6: 46**

> *Jesus expects those who hear the sermon to do what he teaches. He is not presenting an impossible ideal. Nor does he intend his sermon for the chosen few* – **Frank J. Matera**

Against: "SoP" offers broad principles (inspires **Situation Ethics**) but cannot work in practice (e.g. magistrates refusing to judge criminals, bosses unable to criticise employees); some say ethics apply to PRIVATE life not PUBLIC life (**Matera** rejects this)

Marshall's view that "SoP" offers a "broad horizon" for viewing morality

For: Jesus reinterprets Jewish ethics in a broader, more compassionate way (altruism replaces retaliation) → readers have to go beyond Jesus' setting too, apply ideas in new setting

> *we have to go beyond biblical teaching expressed in a specific cultural setting, for example in recognizing that slavery ... is fundamentally at variance with the biblical understanding of man* – **I. Howard Marshall**

Similar to **Situation Ethics** or **Natural Moral Law**: take Biblical PRINCIPLES (not exact rules) and apply them to new situations (e.g. fertility treatment, same sex marriage)

Against: Jesus tells his listeners to *do what he says* – not 'do something inspired by the ideas behind what he says'; danger of 'diluting' Jesus' strict teachings, introducing subjective judgments, making excuses for the people that Jesus condemns (rich, well-fed, laughing, popular)

6.2 ETHICAL PARABLES (Anthology #10)

THE PARABLE OF THE GOOD SAMARITAN (Luke 10: 25-37)

Introduction: Samaritans = rival tribe, religion similar to Judaism, hostility with Jews; Jesus being questioned by a **Pharisee** who claims to keep all the commandants in the Old Testament

Plot: Traveler goes from Jerusalem (mountains) to Jericho (plain); attacked by robbers and left for dead; Jewish priest and Levite (monk) ignore him; **Samaritan** helps him: treats wounds, puts him on donkey, takes him to inn, leaves money for expenses until he returns

Meaning: (1) **moral:** *love your* neighbour = people you don't think of as your neighbour (enemies, other religions) → altruism, not judging; (2) **allegory:** traveler = humanity, priest/Levite = Jewish religion; Samaritan = Christ; donkey = Christ's body on the cross; inn = Christian church; Samaritan's return = *Parousia*

1st century Judaism: *love your neighbour* based on Jewish Scriptures

> *love the Lord your God with all your heart and with all your soul and with all your might?* – **Deuteronomy 6:5**
> *love your neighbour as yourself* – **Leviticus 19: 18**

Jesus UNIVERSALISES the instruction by making *neighbour* mean **anyone** (not just fellow-Jews)

Christian codes of living: founding of hospitals/charities; **Rev. Chad Varah** founded 'The Samaritans' in 1953 (volunteers support depressed and suicidal people through telephone)

Equality today: differences of race, nationality, culture are meaningless compared to the duty to show compassion to fellow human beings

Pluralism today: religious distinctions (= priest and the Levite) are distractions from true duty to love God through loving your neighbour

PARABLES OF THE LOST (Luke 15: 1-32)

Introduction: Pharisees complain that Jesus associates with *sinners* (= publicans, prostitutes, also diseased, perhaps Samaritans)

Plot: (1) shepherd searches for one lost sheep, rejoices when he brings it back; (2) woman searches house for lost coin, throws party when she finds it; (3) son demands early inheritance but squanders it on sinful living, ends up in poverty as a pig-keeper, decides to go home and work for father, father runs out to greet him, throws a party, older son is bitter, father tries to reconcile them both

Meaning: (1) **moral:** God rejoices over lost souls who repent, Jesus = God, searching for lost souls; (2) **allegory:** bitter son = Pharisees, father = God, prodigal (reckless) son = sinners who repent, party = Kingdom of God (Pharisees won't enter as they are too self-righteous)

1st century Judaism: hard-hearted **Phariseeism** vs loving God in a humble spirit; **Form Critics** treat this as a *pericope* (attitudes of 1st century Christians: they are prodigal son, Jews are harrd-hearted older brother)

Christian codes of living: importance of second chances; be delighted when somebody repents BUT dilemmas e.g. sexual misconduct rarely tolerated by early Church, ALSO former-Christians who denied faith during persecutions then wanted to return → distinguishing VENAL sins (forgiven by confessing) vs MORTAL sins → EXCOMMUNICATION from Church

Equality today: historic crimes (slavery, genocide) by entire societies → COLLECTIVE GUILT → NATIONAL REPENTANCE (e.g. Germany compensates Israel for Holocaust; UK Government apologized for slave trade in 2007)

Pluralism today: historic grievances: Crusades (Christians and Muslims), Reformation (Catholics and Protestants) → makes religious tolerance difficult; Catholic Church apologised in 2000 for sins against Jews, heretics, Gypsies and native peoples

THE RICH MAN AND LAZARUS (Luke 16: 19-31)

Introduction: not clear if actually a Parable (don't usually have named characters) or true story; may be based on Egyptian folk tale (**I. Howard Marshall**); Rich Man's name is sometimes Dives (means 'wealth'); Jesus has been warning **Pharisees** that *"you cannot serve both God and money"* (**Luke 16: 13**)

Plot: Rich man lives in luxury while Lazarus begs in the street; both die, Rich Man → *Hades* (Hell), Lazarus → *Abraham's side* (Paradise); Rich Man begs for help but Abraham refuses to help him; asks for Lazarus to be sent to Earth to warn his brothers; Abraham replies people who ignore clear warnings in Scriptures will not listen even if someone comes back from the dead

Meaning: (1) **moral:** link to "SoP" since Rich Man *received his good things in his lifetime* but Lazarus gets comforted in Afterlife; (2) **allegory:** someone coming back from dead = Jesus, brothers who ignore Scriptures = Pharisees or Jews generally who don't believe in Jesus

1st century Judaism: *"they do not listen to Moses and the Prophets"* = Written + Oral Torah (the Scriptures of **Pharisees**) → Pharisees ignore their own Scriptures; teachings about the poor *are* in Old Testament but get *ignored* if religion has no focus on *agape*-love

Christian codes of living: ethical use of wealth (e.g. "SoP" and **Parable of the Good Samaritan**); fail to show love/mercy in *this* life → not receive it from God in Afterlife; faith in Jesus' atoning death/Resurrection means that sins will be forgiven so long as they sincerely tried.

Equality today: economic inequality (vs Christian tendency to focus on sexual sin): Jesus has more to say about wealth than sex; people *cannot serve two masters*: God vs money

Pluralism today: If Jesus (or Luke) adapted (pagan) Egyptian folk tale (as **I. Howard Marshall** suggests) = religious pluralism (we can learn things from other religions too)

> *no one civilization encompasses all the spiritual, ethical and artistic expressions of mankind* – **Jonathan Sacks**, Chief Rabbi (2002)

TOPIC 6 EXAM QUESTIONS & REVISION ACTIVITIES

A-Level Paper 3 (New Testament)

Section A

1. Explore the key ideas in the Sermon on the Plain in Luke 6. (8 marks)

2. Assess the work of **either** Frank Morison **or** Ian Wilson on alternative explanations for the empty tomb. (12 marks)

Section B

Read the following passage before answering the questions.

> **10** On one occasion an expert in the law stood up to test Jesus. "Teacher," he asked, "what must I do to inherit eternal life?"
>
> 26 "What is written in the Law?" he replied. "How do you read it?"
>
> 27 He answered, "'Love the Lord your God with all your heart and with all your soul and with all your strength and with all your mind; and, 'Love your neighbour as yourself.'"
>
> 28 "You have answered correctly," Jesus replied. "Do this and you will live."
>
> 29 But he wanted to justify himself, so he asked Jesus, "And who is my neighbour?"
>
> 30 In reply Jesus said: "A man was going down from Jerusalem to Jericho, when he was attacked by robbers. They stripped him of his clothes, beat him and went away, leaving him half dead. 31 A priest happened to be going down the same road, and when he saw the man, he passed by on the other side. 32 So too, a Levite, when he came to the place and saw him, passed by on the other side. 33 But a Samaritan, as he travelled, came where the man was; and when he saw him, he took pity on him. 34 He went to him and bandaged his wounds, pouring on oil and wine. Then he put the man on his own donkey, brought him to an inn and took care of him. 35 The next day he took out two *denarii* and gave them to the innkeeper. 'Look after him,' he said, 'and when I return, I will reimburse you for any extra expense you may have.'
>
> 36 "Which of these three do you think was a neighbour to the man who fell into the hands of robbers?"
>
> 37 The expert in the law replied, "The one who had mercy on him."
>
> Jesus told him, "Go and do likewise."
>
> Quote from New International Translation, Luke 10: 25-37

3   (a) Clarify the ideas illustrated in this passage about the teaching of Jesus in relation to Judaism at the time. *You must refer to the passage in your response.* **(10 marks)**

(b) Assess the claim that Jesus' teachings guide how Christians should live today. **(20 marks)**

Section C

4   Evaluate the view that the Resurrection was just an event in the experience of the disciples.

Evaluate this view in the context of scientific challenges to the Resurrection. In your response to this question, you must include how developments in New Testament Studies have been influenced by one of the following:

- Philosophy of Religion
- Religion and Ethics
- the study of a religion.

(30 marks)

Total = 90 marks

In these example papers, all the questions are drawn from Topic 6. A real exam would not be like this and each question would probably draw from a different Topic instead.

Comprehension Quiz

1. What is meant by the Resurrection?
2. Given an example of a similarity between two Gospel accounts of the empty tomb
3. What is Swoon Theory?
4. What is the myth of a dying-and-rising god?
5. Explain why the Resurrection is unlikely to be a hallucination
6. What is the 'priestly plot' in Matthew's Gospel??
7. Why is it irrational to believe in miracles according to David Hume?
8. What is the Golden Rule?
9. In what way is the Sermon on the Plain aimed at Gentiles?
10. Who were the Samaritans?
11. Why did the Priest and the Levite ignore the wounded traveler?
12. In what sense does the Parable of the Lost Son illustrate the problem with Pharisees?
13. What two favours does Lazarus beg from Abraham?
14. Why does Abraham refuse him?
15. What is meant by pluralism?

Bible Quotes to match

Explain how each quote links to this Topic

1. *"Why do you call me, 'Lord, Lord,' and do not do what I say?"* – **Luke 6: 46**
2. *"But woe to you who are rich, for you have already received your comfort"* – **Luke 6: 24**
3. *"Do to others as you would have them do to you"* – **Luke 6: 31**
4. *love the Lord your God with all your heart and with all your soul and with all your might* – **Deuteronomy 6:5**
5. *"You cannot serve both God and money"* – **Luke 16: 13**
6. *if Christ has not been raised, our preaching is useless and so is your faith* – **1 Corinthians 15: 14**
7. *"love your enemies, do good to those who hate you"* – **Luke 6: 27**
8. *And beginning with Moses and all the Prophets, he explained to them what was said in all the Scriptures concerning himself* – **Luke 24: 27**

A-Level Year 2 New Testament Studies

Word Search

Find 20 terms/names from this Topic and explain them

```
T E B G Y R S O P S H B E H N
S N L E N E L E A T T G T Y J
L R E B A H N M R H Y X A P S
O J Z M A T A O L E M R N O H
R I P D N R I Y M F M S I C K
T N E F I E A T L T I M C R S
C S K T I Q T P U N M N U I U
U X A G B H Z H O D O I L S R
V N W R I Z E I G I E S L Y A
S E R M O N L K S I S I A S Z
M D E L C A R I M J L W H E A
T P H B T X V G J M W N O W L
F D M X W O E R Q Q A X E O R
V O E G O L D E N R U L E U N
T L P L Y J T I U R F I H O K
```

Crossword

Across
2. Careless with money
3. Destination for the traveler who was attacked by robbers
5. Theory that Jesus did not die on the cross
9. Joseph who provided the tomb came from here
11. David who destroyed the Swoon Hypothesis
14. Jewish prophet believed to be immortal
15. _____ Magdalene who found the empty tomb
17. Name of the Rich Man according to tradition
18. Violation of the laws of nature
19. Roman empress who found the site of Jesus' tomb

Down
1. _____ Rule, do as you would be done to
2. Location of the sermon in Luke 6
4. Someone whose actions do not match their words
6. A blessing
7. _____ disorder, a mental condition that might explain the Resurrection sightings
8. David who argued it's irrational to believe in miracles
10. Jewish sect that could have helped Jesus survive crucifixion
12. Dying-and-_____ god
13. Tribe of people hated by 1st century Jews
16. A non-physical experience sent by God

55

Debates in this Topic

Indicate where you stand on this debate by marking a cross on the line then list points in favour and points against your position (more in favour the closer to the edge, more against the closer to the middle)

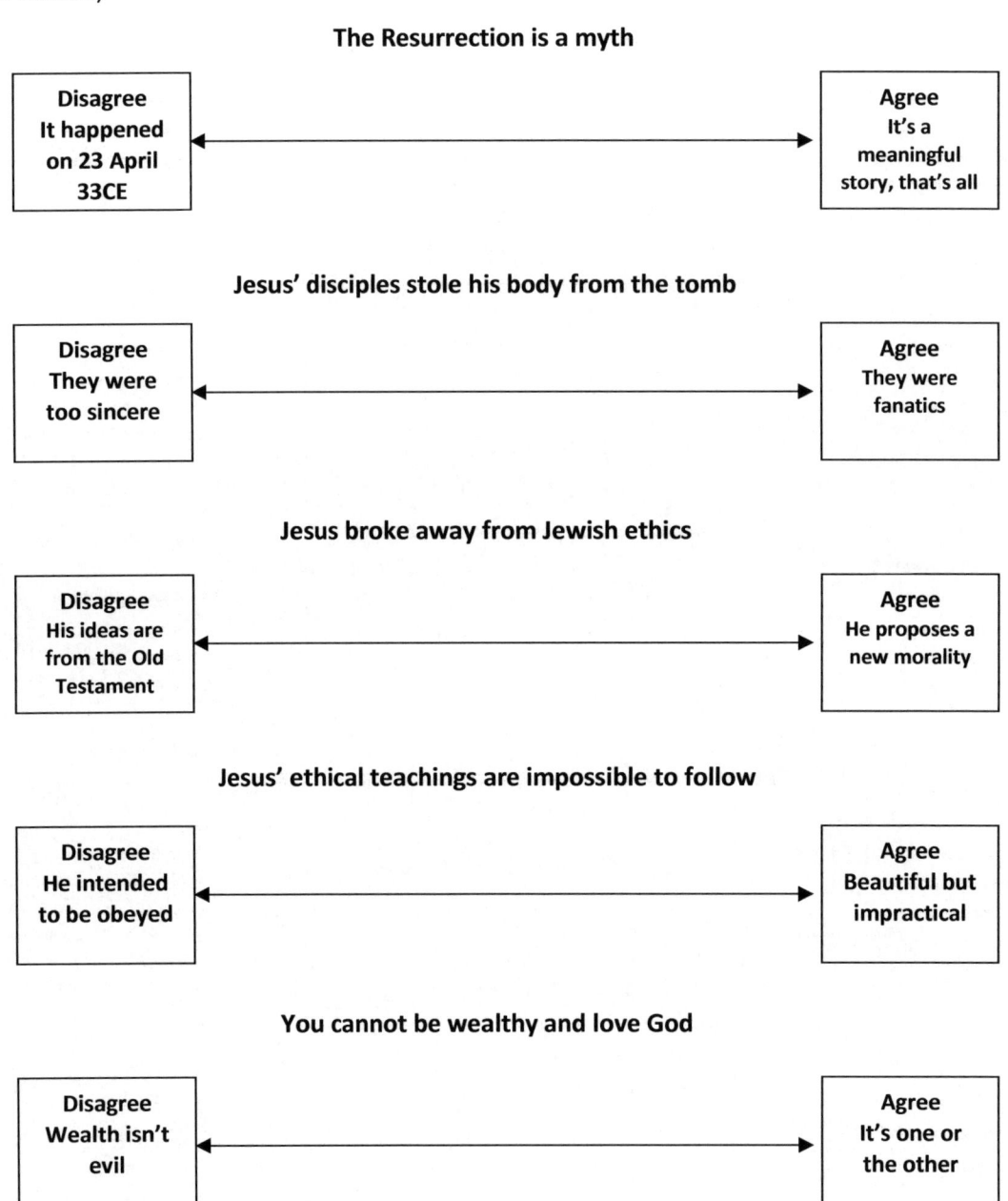

The Resurrection is a myth

| Disagree
It happened on 23 April 33CE | ←——————————→ | Agree
It's a meaningful story, that's all |

Jesus' disciples stole his body from the tomb

| Disagree
They were too sincere | ←——————————→ | Agree
They were fanatics |

Jesus broke away from Jewish ethics

| Disagree
His ideas are from the Old Testament | ←——————————→ | Agree
He proposes a new morality |

Jesus' ethical teachings are impossible to follow

| Disagree
He intended to be obeyed | ←——————————→ | Agree
Beautiful but impractical |

You cannot be wealthy and love God

| Disagree
Wealth isn't evil | ←——————————→ | Agree
It's one or the other |

Cloze Exercise

People have proposed _____ alternatives to the Resurrection right from the beginning. _____'s Gospel describes a rumour put around by the Jewish priests that the Disciples stole Jesus' body from the tomb. _____ points out that the Gospels seem to have been written specifically to counter some explanations, such as the Disciples touching the Risen Jesus (to show he wasn't a _____) or the _____ at the Crucifixion carefully noting where Jesus was buried (to show they didn't go to the wrong tomb).

These criticisms gained force from the new rationalist and _____ mentality of the Enlightenment, with its focus on scientific rather than _____ explanations. _____ argues that, since miracles are the most _____ events, even really unlikely explanations are more probable than miraculous explanations.

One of these explanations was the _____, which is that Jesus did not die on the cross but revived in the tomb (perhaps with help from the _____ sect) and his recovery was mistaken for a miracle by his ignorant Disciples.

However, there are criticisms of all these alternatives. _____ argues that the Disciples do not seem to be the sort of people who would lie about the Resurrection or suffer persecution for something they knew to be a hoax. _____ argues that, if Jesus survived crucifixion, he would have been horribly injured and could not have convinced his followers he was the 'David Strauss _____ of life' who had conquered death. Even Hume has been accused of _____, since he assumes miracles don't happen and uses this to prove that miracles can't happen.

Separate from the question of Jesus' miraculous Resurrection is the issue of his ethical teaching. This is summed up in his Sermon on the _____ in Luke 6. Jesus pronounces a series of blessings (or _____) on people who are currently poor, _____, weeping or hated and abused. He predicts woes or suffering for those who are rich, well-fed, laughing and popular. This link with the arrival of the _____ when there will be a reversal of positions. It also contains a coded criticism of Judaism and predictions of his own death and Resurrection.

Jesus urges his followers to forgive their enemies and show them love rather than hate. He advises followers not to judge anyone for their sins and warns against the dangers of _____, which means claiming to be good when you are not.

Jesus illustrates his teachings with parables such as the _____, where a wounded man is shown love by someone who ought to hate him. In another Parable, the sinful son who _____ is shown forgiveness, but the _____ are compared to the dutiful but bitter son who does not show love for his brother. Finally, the story of the Rich Man and _____ illustrates Jesus' sermon, because after death people's roles are _____, which encourages those who are lucky in this life to help the poor.

Beatitudes, circular logic, David Hume, David Strauss, Essene, Frank Morison, Good Samaritan, hallucination, hungry, hypocrisy, Ian Wilson, improbable, Kingdom of God, Lazarus, Matthew, naturalistic, Plain, Pharisees, Prince, repents, reversed, sceptical, supernatural, Swoon Hypothesis, women

YEAR 2 EXAM PRACTICE PAPER

A-Level Paper 3 (New Testament)

Section A

1   Explore the key ideas about the arrival of the Kingdom of God in the present. (8 marks)

2   Assess the work of **either** Karl Barth **or** Rudolf Bultmann on the value of Scripture. (12 marks)

Section B

Read the following passage before answering the questions.

Jesus Sentenced to Be Crucified

19 Then Pilate took Jesus and had him flogged. ² The soldiers twisted together a crown of thorns and put it on his head. They clothed him in a purple robe ³ and went up to him again and again, saying, "Hail, king of the Jews!" And they slapped him in the face.

⁴ Once more Pilate came out and said to the Jews gathered there, "Look, I am bringing him out to you to let you know that I find no basis for a charge against him." ⁵ When Jesus came out wearing the crown of thorns and the purple robe, Pilate said to them, "Here is the man!"

⁶ As soon as the chief priests and their officials saw him, they shouted, "Crucify! Crucify!"

But Pilate answered, "You take him and crucify him. As for me, I find no basis for a charge against him."

⁷ The Jewish leaders insisted, "We have a law, and according to that law he must die, because he claimed to be the Son of God."

⁸ When Pilate heard this, he was even more afraid, ⁹ and he went back inside the palace. "Where do you come from?" he asked Jesus, but Jesus gave him no answer. ¹⁰ "Do you refuse to speak to me?" Pilate said. "Don't you realize I have power either to free you or to crucify you?"

¹¹ Jesus answered, "You would have no power over me if it were not given to you from above. Therefore the one who handed me over to you is guilty of a greater sin."

¹² From then on, Pilate tried to set Jesus free, but the Jewish leaders kept shouting, "If you let this man go, you are no friend of Caesar. Anyone who claims to be a king opposes Caesar."

Quote from New International Translation, John 19: 1-12

3   (a) Clarify the ideas illustrated in this passage about why the religious and political authorities were so concerned about Jesus. *You must refer to the passage in your response.* (10 marks)

(b) Analyse the claim that it was the Roman imperial system that killed Jesus. (20 marks)

Section C

4   "Jesus' ethics are idealistic but not practical"

Evaluate this view in the context of how we should live, including religious and secular views. In your response to this question, you must include how developments in New Testament Studies have been influenced by one of the following:

- Philosophy of Religion
- Religion and Ethics
- the study of a religion.

(30 marks)

Total = 90 marks

In this example paper, all the questions are drawn from Topics 4-6. A real A-Level exam would probably also draw from Topics 1-3 as well.

ABOUT THE AUTHOR

Jonathan Rowe is a teacher of Religious Studies, Psychology and Sociology at Spalding Grammar School and he creates and maintains **www.philosophydungeon.weebly.com** for Edexcel Religious Studies and **www.psychologywizard.net** for Edexcel A-Level Psychology. He has worked as an examiner for various Exam Boards but is not affiliated with Edexcel. This series of books grew out of the resources he created for his students. Jonathan also writes novels and creates resources for his hobby of fantasy wargaming. He likes warm beer and smooth jazz.

Printed in Great Britain
by Amazon